Contents

BUILDING YOUR
WORKSHOP

BUILDING & OUTFITTING YOUR
WORKSHOP

BY DON MCNAIR

 **TAB BOOKS Inc.**
BLUE RIDGE SUMMIT, PA. 17214

FIRST EDITION

FIRST PRINTING

Copyright © 1983 by TAB BOOKS Inc.
Printed in the United States of America

Library of Congress Cataloging in Publication Data

McNair, Don, 1938-
Building and outfitting your workshop.
Includes index.
1. Workshops. I. Title.
TT152.M4   1983   684'.08   83-4894
ISBN 0-8306-0547-9
ISBN 0-8306-1547-4 (pbk.)

Introduction

IF YOU'RE LIKE ME, YOU LIKE TO BUILD THINGS. YOU READ ABOUT IT, think about it, and talk about it. If you're fortunate enough to have the space and proper equipment, you can do something about it.

If you're like me, you're also frustrated by not having the right environment and tools with which to make your dream projects possible. The "how to" books we buy often frustrate us even more. Some show pictures of utopian, expensive, and often impractical workshop layouts, tease us with what might be, and then often don't follow through with the hard how-to-do-it information we need to make the dreams reality. So we dream some more, shrug our shoulders, lay the books aside, and go to some other activity.

It was from these very same frustrations that this book, featuring 26 projects I have built, was developed. A technical person by profession (I write how-to articles for clients and work with editors of trade magazines to get them placed, and I was once a technical illustrator for a major corporation), I had long dreamed of making my own "ideal" workshop. For years I read all the dream books I could find and began developing my own ideas of what the ideal shop should consist. When I finally acquired the space I needed for a workshop, I was finally able to put those pigeon-holed thoughts into action.

The result was a *complete* shop that works—and one which you can build, too! I was fortunate enough to have use of a two-car garage and I could spread my ideas over a good-sized area. But you can build and install exactly the same type of equipment in a much smaller space. The projects are designed for efficient use of space; remember, I had the projects in mind well before I knew how much space I could devote to them. By building them, you'll be able to make more efficient use of your own space than you ever dreamed possible.

These projects break down logically into four general areas: the work area, storage, work-center tools and fixtures, and accessories. These areas make up the four sections of this book. I will be the first to admit that, just as logically, some projects can be classified in more than one of the areas. For example, is a workbench part of the work area or is it a tool or fixture? I opted for the former. A rack for special fixtures is storage in the strict sense, but I put it with the fixtures because it just seemed to make more sense. And so on.

Where should you start? First, thumb through the pages to become familiar with the contents—then indulge yourself. Start where *you* prefer. Whatever looks fun, and most useful at the moment, should be first. Put your own dream shop together in your own way so that you can use it with pride for many years. Enjoy!

A Few
Words about Tools

I F YOU ARE CONSIDERING OUTFITTING A WORKSHOP, YOU UN-
doubtedly have most, if not all, the tools you'll need with which
to do it. Surprised? Well, just think about what tools you do have. A
hammer? Screwdrivers? Measuring tape or yardstick? An electric
drill? These are among the most commonly used tools needed to
build the projects described in this book (see Tools Needed for
Projects chart on page x); odds are you already have them on hand.

A saw is needed for each of these projects. Here we get into a
matter of personal choices, and perhaps a make-do situation. I swear
by my radial-arm saw. Even the simplest cutting job for these
projects can be done with it, although a table saw, a circular saw, or
even a handsaw will accomplish the tasks.

Although the versatility of a higher class of saw might make it
appear to be the only choice, as soon as such a statement is made, a
skillful craftsman with a trusty handsaw will undoubtedly prove it
wrong. The ingenuity of the home craftsman is amazing, and that is
precisely why only "saw" or "scroll saw" are listed in the "Project
Tools" tables.

In some cases, the versatility of one tool will eliminate the
need of another. As an example, a router is listed as needed for 14 of
the 26 projects, but it will not be needed for several of them if you
prefer to make dadoes and grooves with a power saw. The router is
an important tool. With one, you'll find your projects often turn out
looking better and that you can make sophisticated projects.

Tools Needed for Projects.

Project number	1	2	3	4	5	6	7	8	9	10	11	12	13
Saw	X	X	X	X	X	X	X	X	X	X	X	X	X
Hammer	X	X	X	X	X	X	X	X	X	X	X	X	
Screwdriver	X	X	X			X		X		X	X		X
Square	X	X	X		X	X				X	X	X	
Expandable bit	X							X					
Countersink bit	X	X	X			X							X
Router	X	X		X		X			X	X			X
Drill	X	X	X	X		X			X		X	X	X
Scroll saw		X			X	X							
Diagonal pliers		X											
Clamps		X				X							X
Adjustable wrench		X		X		X							
Measuring tape	X	X	X	X	X	X	X	X	X	X	X	X	X
Level			X						X				
Utility knife			X										
Pliers		X		X		X							
Molding blade													
Protractor													

Project number	14	15	16	17	18	19	20	21	22	23	24	25	26
Saw	X	X	X	X	X	X	X	X	X	X	X	X	X
Hammer		X		X	X	X		X	X	X	X	X	X
Screwdriver		X		X			X	X		X			X
Square			X	X			X						X
Expandable bit													
Countersink bit			X	X			X			X	X		
Router	X	X	X			X				X	X		
Drill	X	X	X	X		X	X	X		X	X		X
Scroll saw													
Diagonal pliers													
Clamps		X	X	X	X	X				X		X	X
Adjustable wrench		X											
Measuring tape	X	X	X	X	X	X	X	X	X	X	X	X	X
Level													
Utility knife													
Pliers	X		X			X			X				
Molding blade				X									
Protractor												X	

Another frequently useful instrument is the carpenter's square. This is an invaluable yet inexpensive tool, and it should certainly be close at hand in any workshop. Often it can be interchanged with a try square, and indeed, only the carpenter's square is mentioned in the "Project Tools" tables in this book. The costs are so minor and the convenience of having just the right tools when you need them is so compelling that you should have one of each.

A few specialty tools are listed. If you don't have them you can often make do. Example? An expandable bit can often be replaced by drilling a smaller hole and enlarging it with a scroll saw. A wood chisel can be used to remove stock that otherwise would be removed with succeeding passes of a radial-arm saw. Adjustable wrenches and pliers are generally exchangeable in this book, and in many other projects in which you might become involved.

In specific cases, the diagonal pliers (used to cut and strip wire) called for in Project 2, can be replaced by a utility knife or another cutting instrument. The molding blade in Project 17 can certainly be replaced by a scroll saw, although the resulting cut might not turn out as pretty. The molding blade is recommended because the auxiliary table being constructed is made for use of that attachment.

By selecting certain projects to do first, you can make the tools that are required for others. The water levels in Project 22, for instance, can accomplish leveling work needed in Projects 3 and 9. The tapering jig in Project 19 is needed for Project 7, and so on.

Perhaps the best approach to tools, at this point, is to realize that by outfitting your shop you are committing yourself to using certain tools, whether you have the proper ones now or not. Now might be the time to acquire that radial saw and that router. It will certainly make project construction easier, and it will give you a head start on the enjoyable use of your workshop for many years to come.

1
Work Area

JUST AS A MANUFACTURER NEEDS A FACTORY IN WHICH TO PRO-
duce goods, you need space and services in order to accomplish your work. You cannot conveniently build many projects in a
bedroom or on the lawn outside, as extreme examples, without
running into spouse or weather problems.

You probably have space in mind in which to build projects. It
could be in the attic, basement, garage, or an unfinished room.
Congratulations! Many would-be craftsmen don't even have this
type of minimal space and they are destined to dream about the day
when they will have it.

Think about the space that you do have. Is it adequate now for
what you really want to do there? Do you have proper surfaces to
work on, power to work with, and good light to see by? Is it the right
temperature throughout the year for comfortable use or will you, by
necessity, become a warm-weather hobbyist?

The answers to such questions are the subject of this chapter.
Included are five projects that will help you convert raw space into a
usable workshop. With this accomplished, you'll note a tremendous
improvement in your enjoyment of whatever craft you pursue, and
you may even find an improvement in the finished projects themselves. If you are a serious home craftsman, you'll undoubtedly see
the logic of getting your own "factory" ready so you can enjoy your
hobby just that much more. These are proven ways to help you do it!

PROJECT 1: MOVEABLE WORKBENCH

Quickly: what is the single most important construction project for the home workshop?

If you said "workbench," you probably are in a plurality. The workbench has traditionally been considered the center of most workshop activity. Although craftsmen certainly do—or, at least, *should* do—some chores in other parts of the shop, they do have a tendency to return to this base of operations.

If you think about it, the traditional workbench often leaves much to be desired. Too often it is a one-purpose object that at times seems to block your attempts to use it in other ways that appear logical. When you occasionally think how handy it would be in another location, even for just a few moments, it glowers at you—defying you to move its bulk even an inch.

If you dare to attach a vise, the vise immediately gets in your way for projects requiring flat areas. And storage? Too often, that neat, under-the-table area is just the wrong size or shape to be of much use. It soon becomes cluttered with scrap, little-used equipment, and half-finished and eventually forgotten projects. In short, the sweetheart of the shop—or what should be, at any rate—too often becomes the wallflower. Its take-me-or-leave-me attitude undoubtedly encourages some would-be suitors—perhaps yourself on occasion—to look elsewhere for some at-home enjoyment.

This needn't be the case, however, as the workbench featured in this project aptly illustrates (Fig. 1-1). The bench was aggressively designed to eliminate these very problems while retaining the workbench features most needed: size (almost 8 feet long), a solid top, and sturdy construction that invites frequent and rough use.

Notice that the bench is mounted on heavy-duty casters, two of them lockable, that allow you to move the bench to any place in the shop in order to tackle jobs where they are located. This means you can put the bench in the center of the floor and work all around it, rather than just from one side.

It also has a built-in, hide-away vise that provides a third hand when it is needed. When it is *not* needed, you fold the vise under the table surface. Its jaws can be positioned almost 8 feet apart. One jaw can be used as a bench stop while the other is tucked away.

The space beneath the bench top also works for you. One large area features adjustable shelves behind double doors. A same-size area at the other end has no floor or bottom framework. This allows you to roll your vacuum sweeper, waste bin, and other such objects out of sight. A portable tool caddy, Project 8, will also fit this space.

The Framework

The total framework is made up of 2×4s. Select your material

Fig. 1-1. This attractive, 8-foot long workbench has a solid top, a bench stop, ample storage space and—due to its large casters—easy portability.

Table 1-1. Project 1 Tools.

| Saw |
| Hammer |
| Screwdriver |
| Square |
| Expandable Bit |
| Countersink Bit |
| Router |
| Drill |
| Measuring Tape |

carefully and use only straight, quality lumber. Pre-cut lodge pole studs were used for the workbench.

To speed your work, cut all parts of the framework before any assembly takes place. See Tables 1-1, 1-2, and Fig. 1-2. Dimensions for boards requiring special cutting are shown in Fig. 1-3. Other boards need only be cut to length.

Construct the top part of the frame first as shown in Fig. 1-4. Lay the two parts A on the floor, side by side with lap cuts up. Lay the four B parts across them in the lap cuts, positioned so that 2 inches at each end of each B piece overhangs its A piece. Check for squareness, and nail two nails through B and A at each point.

Next make four U-shaped frame assemblies, all but one consisting of two G and one E part. The exception is the frame for the right end of the workbench (as one faces it when it is in its finished form). This frame consists of one G, one E, and the H part, which is identical to the G except that it has no lap cut on the bottom.

Complete the four subassemblies by nailing F parts into place, as shown in Fig. 1-2.

Note that you can vary the bench height by changing the length of G parts. The 29-inch length provides a height of 36 inches (with a ¾-inch plywood top), the height of the radial-arm saw used in its construction. This allows the workbench to serve as a sawing support.

Turn the top assembly over, so that the top surfaces of the four B parts are touching the floor, and invert the left-end subassembly. Place it on the top frame so that the lap joints are located outside

Table 1-2. Framework Materials List.

Part	Dimensions	Quantity	Notes
A	1½″ × 3½″ × 89″	2	
B	1½″ × 3½″ × 28″	4	
C	1½″ × 3½″ × 89″	1	
D	1½″ × 3½″ × 53¾″	1	
E	1½″ × 3½″ × 21″	4	
F	1½″ × 3½″ × 17″	6	
G	1½″ × 3½″ × 29″	7	See Fig. 1-3
H	1½″ × 3½″ × 29″	1	See Fig. 1-3
I	1½″ × 3½″ × 22″	1	
J	1½″ × 1½″ × 22″	1	
K	1½″ × 3½″ × 5″	1	See Fig. 1-3
L (wheels)	4″ diameter	4	All casters must swivel; two must be lockable

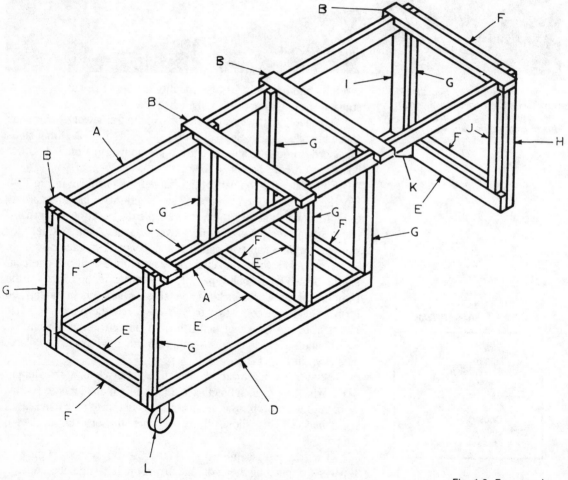

Fig. 1-2. Framework.

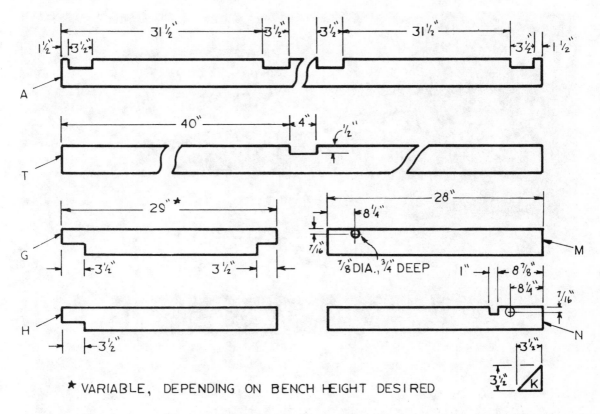

★ VARIABLE, DEPENDING ON BENCH HEIGHT DESIRED

Fig. 1-3. Special cuts.

part B, and its cross member E is on the inside (it will later serve as a flooring support).

Insert the other subassemblies in a similar manner (Figs. 1-5 and 1-6). Refer to Fig. 1-1 for exact positioning. Note, for example, that part E is on the *left* side of the other three subassemblies, and that the two middle subassemblies are on the *inside* of the two middle B parts. Figure 1-7 shows the framework when subassemblies are in place.

Finish the frame by installing parts I, J, and K. Notice that the back surface of J lines up with the back surface of H; this leaves a lip area into which the right-hand door will eventually fit. Be sure the right end of the frame is square with the back, lower frame (piece C) before nailing part K—which is simply a "right triangle" cut from a 2×4—into place. This will assure that the doors will hang properly when installed. Now install the casters, one 4 inches from each corner of the frame, and turn the unit over so that it rests on its wheels.

The Bench Top

The bench top can be made with or without the internal vise, depending upon your preferences and needs. The following instruc-

5

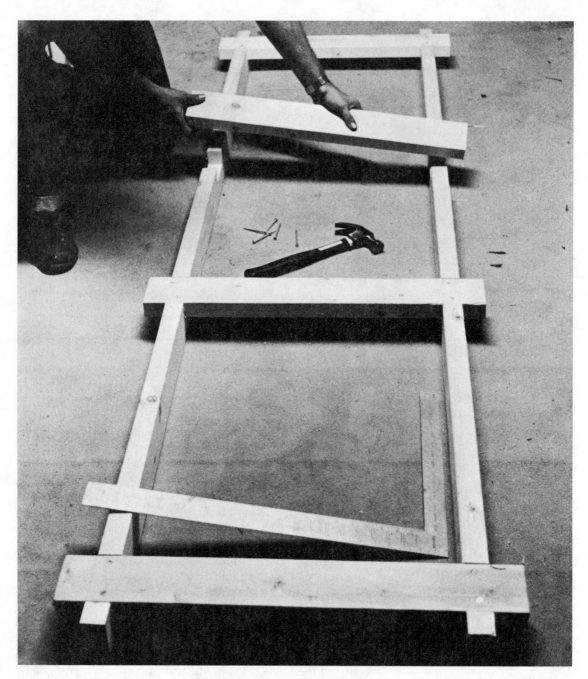

tions first detail the "without" top and then describe the addition of the vise. See Table 1-3.

Making the top is simple. After cutting the parts to size, place one of the W parts at the back on the ends of the four B parts so its back edge is flush with their ends and its own ends are flush with the

Fig. 1-4. The top of frame comes first. Assemble it on the floor while taking care to measure and square it carefully.

Fig. 1-5. Build the frame subassembly and insert into top assembly as shown. Note that the top frame has been turned over.

ends of the bench framework (see Fig. 1-8). Drive two nails through each W-B juncture, and additional nails downward into the W-A edge. Now, one by one, place the next W parts and the T parts into position as shown in Fig. 1-8 and nail them to the B's in a like

Fig. 1-6. Note the frame nailing pattern. This approach guarantees a solid table.

manner. Note that part T is identical to part W, except for the notch that will provide a "home" for the vise when it is not used (Fig. 1-9).

If you plan to build in the vise, put a piece of scrap 2×4 longways on each end part B, next to part T, to serve as a "spacekeeper" (Fig. 1-10). Put the next W part next to them, and nail it and the other part W into place as before. The last W part should be flush with the front ends of cross pieces B.

Now put the two X parts in place, against the sides of the first and last W parts, and centered lengthwise so that they extend 1½ inches at each end. If you are not building the vise, you need not make the special cuts on parts M and N; just cut them to length and place each against the ends of the Ws, between the ends of the Xs, and nail into place.

Now measure the length and width of the surface and cut a top that exact size from a piece of ½-inch or ¾-inch AC plywood (½-inch plywood was used in building this project). Nail it into place, countersinking the nails below the surface. Use wood putty to cover the holes and then sand the spots smooth.

To install the glue clamp and ¾-inch iron pipe, which will become your in-the-bench vise and stop, follow the above steps until installing parts M and N. Use an expandable bit to drill a ⅞-inch hole halfway through each one, as shown in Fig. 1-3, to allow the inserted pipe to turn easily. Notice that the top edge of the hole is even with the surface of parts M and N. Cut the inch-square notch out in part N to receive the clamp's twist handle.

Nail part N into place. Put the glue clamp on the ¾-inch pipe and insert the proper end of that assembly—the one with the twist handle—into the drilled hole (Fig. 1-11). Place the other end of the pipe into the hole in part M, and nail part M in place; you might want to use just a couple of nails at this point so that the part can be removed easily if necessary to make adjustments.

Final nailing of both M and N will include nails through both ends of the X pieces, nails through M and N into the ends of the W pieces, and nails downward through plywood-top pieces Q and S. Make sure that the pipe will swivel easily in these end pieces. You might have to gouge out a small area of the right-end B piece to allow the clamp's lip to turn its full arc.

When you are satisfied with the vise action, it is time to attach

Fig. 1-7. The frame, still upside down, is almost finished. Take care in nailing because some nail heads will be seen after job is finished.

Table 1-3. Bench Top Materials List.

Part	Material	Dimensions	Quantity	Notes
M	2 × 4	1½″ × 3½″ × 28″	1	See Fig. 1-3
N	2 × 4	1½″ × 3½″ × 28″	1	See Fig. 1-3
O	black pipe	¾″ × 91½″	1	
P	gluing clamp	¾″	1	
Q	AC plywood	½″ or ¾″ × 92″ × 18¼″	1	
R	AC plywood	½″ or ¾″ × 92″ × 5″	1	
S	AC plywood	½″ or ¾″ × 92″ × 7½″	1	
T	2 × 4	1½″ × 3½″ × 89″	1	See Fig. 1-3
U	1 × 2	½″ × 1½″ × 82″	1	
V	2 × 2	1½″ × 1½″ × 44″	1	
W	2 × 4	1½″ × 3½″ × 89″	7	
X	2 × 4	1½″ × 3½″ × 92″	2	
Y	2 × 2	1½″ × 1½″ × 36½″	1	

the top plywood surface. Cut Q, R, and S to the dimensions given, and nail pieces Q and S to the W and X pieces. Part Q is to be flush with the back surface of the "back" part X, and S is to be flush with the front surface of the front part X. Before nailing, make sure that there is clearance between them for part R to fit. This way it can be removed and replaced without binding. Notice in Fig. 1-12 that each edge is to rest on a 2×4.

Place part R into position now, noting at what points material must be removed so that it will lie flush with the rest of the bench top (see Fig. 1-12). You probably will have to make adjustments at the right end, over the main part of the clamp, and at the center where the other clamp part rests when the cover is on (see Fig. 1-12). Remove only as much material as you need because its removal from the center of a ½-inch thick top piece will weaken the piece and make it difficult to handle before the brace structure is attached.

The brace structure consists of parts U, V, and Y. Place these into position on parts B—between the 2×4s (W and T) and the iron pipe—put glue on their top surfaces, and carefully place R on top. Make sure you space evenly between R and bench top surfaces Q and S, and make sure R remains flat in relation to Q and S. Drive nails through R into the brace pieces (countersinking). Note that part U provides backbone to the assembly, and it and parts V and W fill all the voids not filled by the iron pipe. You can do any shop work on this "lid" that you can do elsewhere on the surface without fear of damaging either the lid or the vise.

As the last step, turn the moveable end of the clamp up, move it to the far left end of the bench (over the B part, touching part M), and lay the lid into place. Mark the lid as needed. Cut out the portion holding the lid up (Fig. 1-13). The lid should be able to remain flat while the vise portion extends up through it, to serve as a bench stop (Fig. 1-14).

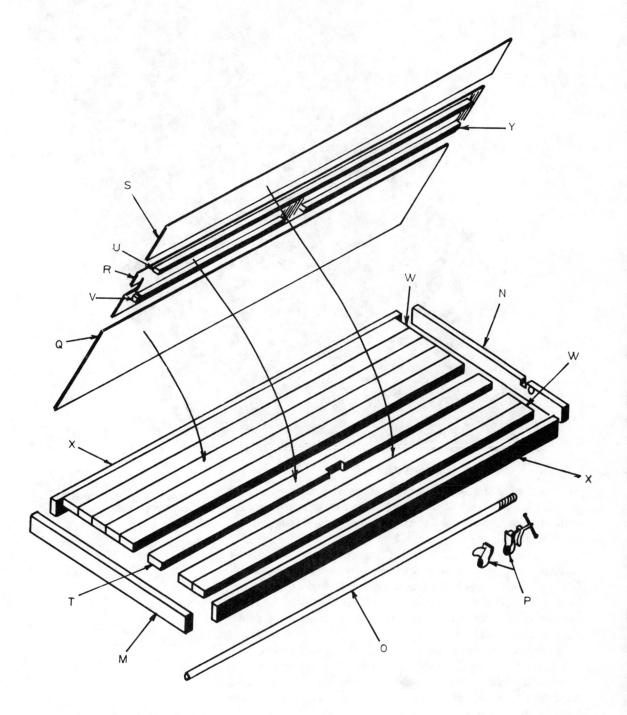

Fig. 1-8. Bench top.

11

Doors and Partitions

The doors add character to your workbench while they accomplish the very laudable goal of protecting its contents. Your doors can certainly look professional if you follow these detailed suggestions. See Table 1-4.

First, notice in Fig. 1-15 that, until the very last possible moment, each pair of front doors is treated as one piece. Cut the left-hand, double-door piece first (according to Fig. 1-15). Be sure to double check the actual sizes of its opening first, however, because slight differences could have cropped up in the building of the framework. Add a half inch to each opening dimension (that is, for each side, top, and bottom) and, if the resulting measurements differ, use those figures instead of the ones in the drawing. Remember that the two double-door openings might vary slightly from each other as well as from the drawing; measure each one individually.

Use a router to make a half-inch wide, ⅜-inch deep rabbet

Fig. 1-10. Place a spacekeeper
2-×-4 piece at each end of the
benchtop frame before nailing part
T into place. This technique
makes sure you "come out even"
with your benchtop boards

completely around the "back" side of the double-door piece (Fig. 1-16). Then turn it over and use a ⅜-inch radius, corner-rounding bit to round edges on the "good" side.

Attach these hinges now; place each one 2 inches from the top (or bottom) on each side of the double-door piece. Now place the piece into the opening, and hold it into that position with a leaning object such as a chair or stool (Fig. 1-17). If you had to force the

piece in, remove the hinges from one side, cut the appropriate amount from the edge, and re-rout both front and back edge surfaces. Then replace it in the bench. There must be a slight space between the door and the cabinet or the finished door will have a tendency to remain ajar. Viewing the door piece from the rear (the back bench panel has not yet been attached), center it both sideways and up and down. Use washers or other small items as spacers.

When you are satisfied with the fitting, it is time to attach the hinges to the bench. With the piece still in position, drill starter holes and install the screws. It is important to do this now—before the piece is sawn in two—because it greatly simplifies alignment.

Remove the screws, carefully measure for and mark the vertical center of the double-door piece, and carefully make that vertical cut to separate the doors. The cuts for the bench featured here were made on a panel saw (Project 6). Now reattach the doors in the drilled screw holes. You'll find that the doors will be straight and that their surface grain matches perfectly.

The right-hand set of doors is prepared in much the same manner (up to and including being attached with screws in the opening). Notice from the drawings and photos, however, that the bottom piece AM, which is a length of 1×4 clear fir, is to be attached to the double door at this point before cutting it into two doors. Measure the opening width and cut AM to fit it closely.

This piece will obviously be slightly shorter than the double-door piece because it does not overlap the frame pieces. Attach it

Fig. 1-12. The cover (right) will turn over into vise cavity, providing a smooth benchtop. Note that some material was removed at the end of the cover in order to clear the vise edge.

with finish nails into the rabbeted edge of AB, Make sure not to nail where the saw will separate the doors. Make that cut now and then attach the doors permanently as described.

Prepare the end door, AC, in a similar manner and attach it to the right end of the workbench. This door will open to reveal a

three-inch deep pegboard-backed cavity designed for storage of tools and accessories (Fig. 1-18). Now attach pull knobs, 10 inches down from the top of each door, and 1½ inches inside the edge.

Except for the shelf, the bottom of the shelf area and pegboard AH, the rest of the pieces are to be made from quarter-inch plywood. Cut all of them at one time in order to save time.

Four pieces—AD, AE, AF, and AG—are of the same size. Pieces AE and AF go inside the shelf area. Each rests on the framework (on parts E), and is centered over the frame end hole and the hole on the opposite side—opposite the drawer cavity. Cut shelf support braces (AL) to length. Make sure their slots line up and then attach them to the framework on each side of parts AE and AF. Insert the shelf support tabs. Cut the ¾-inch plywood shelf(s) and bottom to fit (Fig. 1-19). Now install partition AG and pegboard AH in similar position as AE and AF, at the other end of the bench.

The final pieces are the left end AD, and the back, AN. Round the edges of the "good side" of each with a ¼-inch radius corner-rounding router bit, and attach them to the bench with finish nails. Except for the drawers, the workbench is finished.

Making the Drawers

The drawer fronts were designed to match the height and appear-ance of the double doors on each side. As with the doors, the perimeter routine is to be done on both sides before the piece is cut into the three individual fronts.

Cut the major piece to its overall dimensions (see piece AI in Fig. 1-15, and see also Figs. 1-20 and 1-21) and rout the outside edges as you did the doors. That is, round the front four edges with the ⅜-inch router bit, and rabbet the back, top and bottom, ½ inches wide and ⅜ of an inch deep.

Because the drawer portion itself must be 1 inch narrower than the cabinet drawer opening, to allow for the drawer slides on each side, rabbet the two sides of the piece to a depth of 1⅝ inches. Now, cut the piece into three equal-width horizontal pieces (piece AP in Fig. 1-20) as measured on the front. You will notice that the drawers using the top and bottom fronts will be slightly shallower than the center drawer (because of the top and bottom rabbeting).

It is important to make the drawers as sturdy as possible in order to handle a variety of heavy objects for many years to come. If you have a dovetailing fixture as shown in Project 16, by all means use it. Dovetailing provides one of the strongest drawer joints possible. If you don't have one, and you plan to make projects with drawers later, you might want to invest in the fixture now. If you do not have a fixture, the following system will provide very strong drawers.

Fig. 1-14. Note the smooth top even while the vise is extended upward through lid.

Table 1-4. Doors and Partitions Materials List.

Parts	Material	Dimensions	Quantity
AA	AC plywood	¾" × 34" × 22⅜"	1
AB	AC plywood	¾" × 34" × 22⅜"	1
AC	AC plywood	¾" × 17⅝" × 22⅜"	1
AD	AC plywood	¼" × 18" × 24"	1
AE	AC plywood	¼" × 18" × 24"	1
AF	AC plywood	¼" × 18" × 24"	1
AG	AC plywood	¼" × 18" × 24"	1
AH	Pegboard	¼" × 20" × 24"	1
AI	AC plywood	¾" × 16½" × 22⅜"	1
AJ	Semiconcealed hinges		5 pair
AK	Knobs or handles		5
AL	Shelf supports		2 (cut into 4 pcs)
AM	Clear fir	¾" × 3½" × 33¼"	1
AN	AC plywood	¼" × 88" × 24"	1

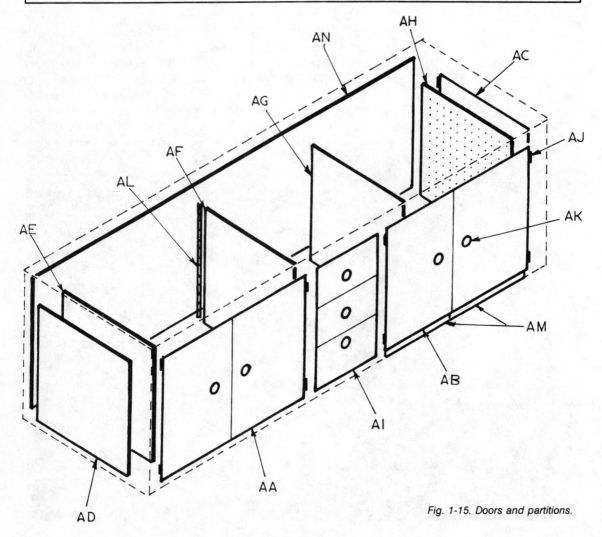

Fig. 1-15. Doors and partitions.

Fig. 1-16. Router table is used to
rout rabbet and radius on door
pieces.

Cut piece AQ for each drawer (Fig. 1-20) so that it is the same
height as the rabbeted portion of the drawer front, and ⅜ of an inch
longer on each side. Glue and screw this piece to the inside of each
front, to provide a lip in order for sides AR and AS to "hold."

Before attaching, drill a hole through AQ to allow passage of

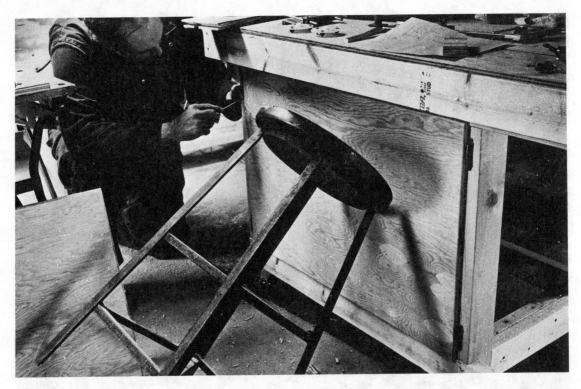

knob or handle screws that are designed to go only through a ¾-inch thick door or drawer front.

The six drawer sides AR and AS are also to remain as one piece until the final moment so that the dados can be made at one time (Fig. 1-21). After separating them, set your radial-arm saw or router to the proper depth to make the grooves in AQ, AR, and AS to receive drawer bottom AU during assembly. Note that AR and AS on each drawer are mirror images. Their grooves are on opposite edges. Make the grooves in AR and AS ⅜ of an inch deep, and the groove in AQ only ⅛ of an inch deep.

To assemble, place one lip of AQ into the proper dado in AR, after putting glue into the dado, and make sure the bottom grooves line up. Drive three or four finish nails through AR at an angle into the front of AP. Do the same with the side AS on the other side, and put the end piece AT into the end dados at the opposite end of the drawer. Make sure its top edge aligns with the top edge of AR and AS, and that its bottom edge is no deeper than the top surface of the drawer bottom grooves; then glue and nail it into place. Use a square throughout to assure a square drawer.

Slip the drawer bottom AU into the grooves from the rear, and make sure it seats properly into the groove in AQ. Put a nail or two up through the bottom into piece AT, but do not glue or nail

Fig. 1-17. Heavy shop bench holds uncut door pair, as hinges are screwed to frame. The panel was later removed and cut in half. Prior hanging assures straight doors.

elsewhere. This allows for seasonal contraction and expansion of the bottom. As a final step, attach the knobs, AV.

To install the drawer slides (Fig. 1-22), follow instructions that accompany them. Insert the bottom set first, then the top, and finally the center. Use screws in only the elongated slots at first, insert drawers, and adjust for proper spacing. After you have "fine-tuned" in this manner, put screws in the other holes for permanent installation.

Your solid, large, versatile, and moveable workbench is now complete. Now comes the fun part. You can start gathering your tools from their various locations, sorting them, and putting them into their new home. You can now "officially" call your work *area* a work*shop*.

Fig. 1-18. Pegboard behind end door provides "free" space for hanging tools and accessories. Opened front door reveals bottomless area designed for rolled-in storage.

Fig. 1-19. Adjustable shelfs will allow you to use this space to your advantage. Although only one shelf is shown, you can use two, three, or even more—depending upon your needs.

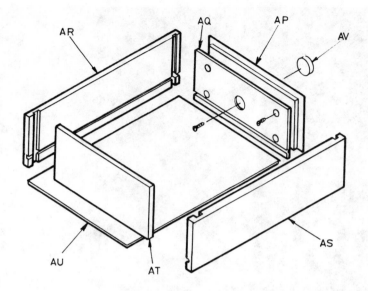

Fig. 1-20. Drawer parts layout.

AR
AQ
AP
AV
AU
AT
AS

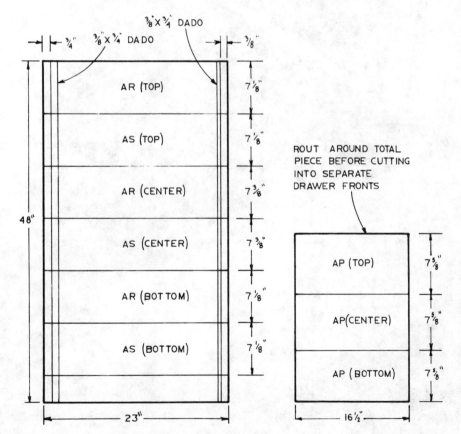

$\frac{3}{8}$" X $\frac{3}{4}$" DADO

$\frac{3}{8}$" X $\frac{3}{4}$" DADO

$\frac{3}{4}$"

$\frac{3}{8}$"

AR (TOP) — 7 $\frac{1}{8}$"

AS (TOP) — 7 $\frac{1}{8}$"

AR (CENTER) — 7 $\frac{3}{8}$"

AS (CENTER) — 7 $\frac{3}{8}$"

AR (BOTTOM) — 7 $\frac{1}{8}$"

AS (BOTTOM) — 7 $\frac{1}{8}$"

48"

23"

ROUT AROUND TOTAL
PIECE BEFORE CUTTING
INTO SEPARATE
DRAWER FRONTS

AP (TOP) — 7 $\frac{5}{8}$"

AP (CENTER) — 7 $\frac{5}{8}$"

AP (BOTTOM) — 7 $\frac{5}{8}$"

16 $\frac{1}{2}$"

Fig. 1-21. Drawers.

Fig. 1-22. Left: Follow manufacturer's instructions to install
drawer slides. Insert the bottom
set and then the top. Fine tune
screws in elongated slots first in
order to determine the correct
position after all slides are in place,
before inserting other screws.

PROJECT 2: LIGHT AND POWER BEAM

"Let there be light . . ." and suddenly our basic lighting needs were taken care of. But that was long before man decided to hide away in little rooms, out of the sun's reach, and while away his time by constructing intricate, eye-straining projects. Even standard overhead house and garage lighting does not fill the bill.

A light and power beam is shown in Figs. 1-23 and 1-24. The 10-foot-long horizontal beam pivots, 180 degrees from the midpoint on a wall, to take efficient fluorescent light directly to the work wherever it might be in that arc (see Figs. 1-23, 1-24, and 1-25). The light fixture—an inexpensive shop light—also traverses the beam and is adjustable up and down on its supporting chains. A switch at the end of the beam turns the light on and off.

To add to this convenience, three grounded, double power receptacles are also featured at the beam's end, and they, too, are switch controlled. This brings power *and* light to any job, and eliminates troublesome extension cords and expensive and often cumbersome duplication of light sources. See Tables 1-5 and 1-6.

Notice that although Figs. 1-26 and 1-27 show the brace assembly in an "up" position for high ceilings, it can be turned down if desired before assembly and mounting, as shown in Fig. 1-25. The

Fig. 1-23. The overhead beam takes light and power to wherever it is needed.

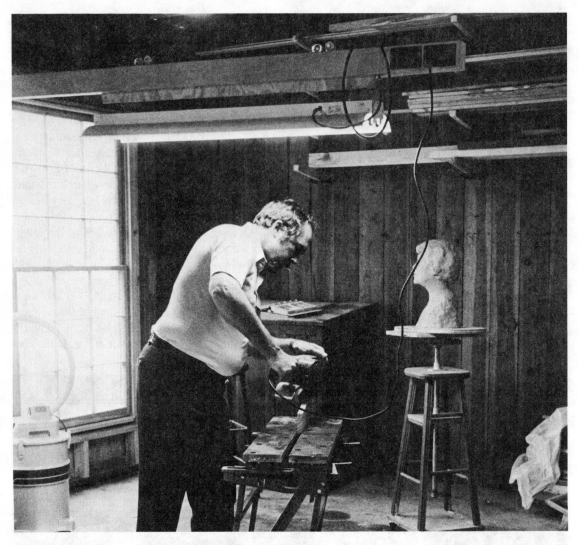

only changes needed are the hinge locations, orientation of the on-off switches, and the direction the power cord exits the beam.

The power beam assembly is made from 1-×-4-inch boards and a single 2-×-4 stud. Speed up the construction by first cutting 1-×-4 pieces to the dimensions given in Fig. 1-28. First cut 45-degree angles on boards D, E, F, G, and H, and then cut each to size. The length of the beam itself, and the length of the upright stud J, can be adjusted to meet requirements in your own shop. Cut the receptacle openings in pieces A and C according to Fig. 1-28.

The power cord is a standard 25-foot, 14-gauge 3-wire extension cord common in the shop. After you have acquired the one you will use, select a router bit one size smaller in diameter to rout the trough shown on board A (see Fig. 1-28). The exact location isn't

Fig. 1-24. A craftsman using an overhead beam at a work center. To work at the bench, he simply swings it around. It also swings in the other direction to provide light and power for floor assembly, craft work, or the drawing board in the background.

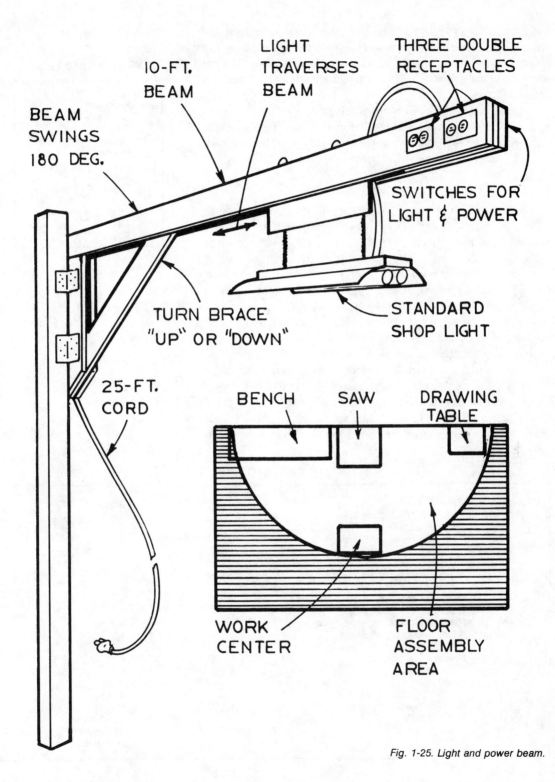

10-FT. BEAM

LIGHT TRAVERSES BEAM

THREE DOUBLE RECEPTACLES

BEAM SWINGS 180 DEG.

SWITCHES FOR LIGHT & POWER

TURN BRACE "UP" OR "DOWN"

STANDARD SHOP LIGHT

25-FT. CORD

BENCH

SAW

DRAWING TABLE

WORK CENTER

FLOOR ASSEMBLY AREA

Fig. 1-25. Light and power beam.

27

crucial as long as the trough ends in the inside receptacle hole already cut. Make the trough deep enough so that the cord can later be pressed into it and cannot be seen above the surface. The cord will deform somewhat; it will take up more depth than a "free" cord does.

At the other end of this board, freehand rout a curve that exists at one side of the board, about 1 inch from the end (Fig. 1-29). While you're using the router, also rout the freehand curve shown in board B, which will later receive the shop light cord.

Wiring

Although wiring the beam might appear difficult from viewing Fig. 1-27, it is actually easy if the following step-by-step directions are followed. The three diagrams in Fig. 1-30 divide the wiring job into three steps, according to the color of the wire.

First, prepare the wires. Cut off the molded power cord receptacle. Carefully remove 10 inches of the cord's outer insulation. Now remove 1 inch of insulation from the end of the three contained wires, thus leaving three exposed ends. Prepare one end of a separate 8-foot cord in the same manner in order to eventually replace the short cord of the shop light.

Lay board A down on a flat surface (with the routed side facing up). Lay the cord along the trough; place the cut end of the cord's outer insulation positioned where the trough enters the receptacle hole. With a scrap piece of lumber, start pushing the cord completely into the trough from that point. Move along the board until

Table 1-5. Project 2 Tools.

Saw
Hammer
Screwdriver
Square
Countersink Bit
Router
Drill
Scroll Saw
Diagonal Pliers
Clamps
Adjustable Wrench
Measuring Tape
Pliers

Table 1-6. Project 2 Bill of Materials.

Material	Quantity
1″ × 4″ × 10′ C-grade fir	4
⅜″ Plywood, 6″ × 48″	1
4″ hinges, brass, with screws	2
3″ lag bolts	3
1″ dia. washers	3
Double receptacle	3
Double switch	1
25′ power cord (14 gauge, 3-wire)	1
8′ cord (16 gauge 3-wire)	1
Hook-up wire (black, white, green)	3 ft. ea.
4-foot. fluorescent shop light	1
Sliding door rollers	4
S-hooks	4
Shop light chain	6 ft.
Screw eye	1
10-32 × ½ machine screws	8
8-gauge ¾ wood screws	8
6d finish nails	24
Wood putty	As needed
White glue	As needed

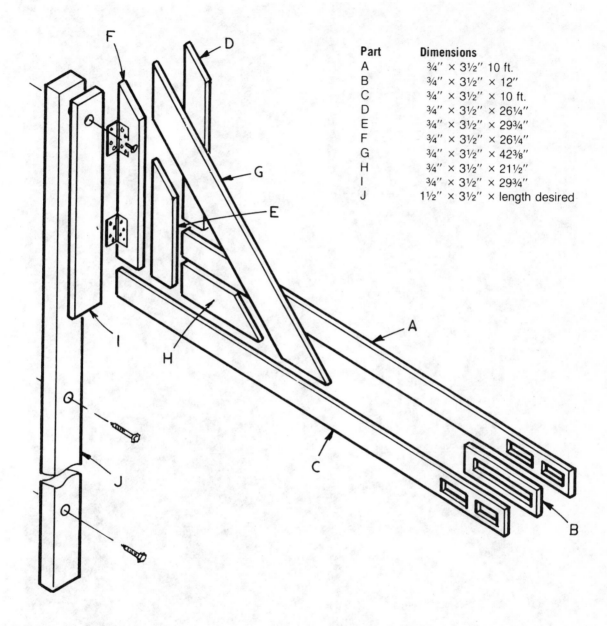

Part	Dimensions
A	¾″ × 3½″ 10 ft.
B	¾″ × 3½″ × 12″
C	¾″ × 3½″ × 10 ft.
D	¾″ × 3½″ × 26¼″
E	¾″ × 3½″ × 29¾″
F	¾″ × 3½″ × 26¼″
G	¾″ × 3½″ × 42⅜″
H	¾″ × 3½″ × 21½″
I	¾″ × 3½″ × 29¾″
J	1½″ × 3½″ × length desired

Fig. 1-26. Beam parts.

reaching the other end (see Fig. 1-28). Now cut 10-inch lengths of insulated 14-gauge wire needed to complete the hook-up (two pieces white, three pieces black, and three pieces green), and strip their ends as you did the power cord wire ends.

To make the hook-up as foolproof as possible, lay out boards A, B, and C as shown in Fig. 1-27. Place the double switch and receptacles face down over their respective holes. After wiring is

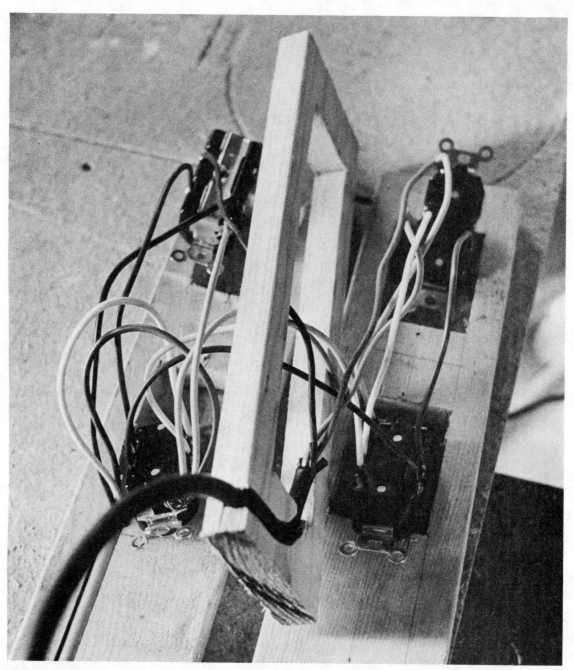

completed, the two outside boards will be "folded up" toward the center board B so that their inside edges will become the bottom of the beam. The double switch is the end unit on the board with the power cord trough (A). It is oriented in the illustration so that the on" position is "up" when the beam brace extends upward. If you

Fig. 1-27. Lay the switch and receptacles in position and wire according to the diagrams shown in Fig. 1-30. Be sure proper wires are routed through the short spacer board.

want your own brace to point down, reverse the switch now.

Refer to the wiring diagrams in Fig. 1-30 and complete the wiring, one color at a time, checking yourself carefully after each color is hooked up. Bend the wire ends clockwise so that the crook tends to tighten as the screw is driven home. Note: green is the grounding wire. If your switch has no grounding screw, attach the wire to the switch's metal frame. Be sure the appropriate wires are properly positioned through piece B, and that all screws—both those used and those not used—are tightened.

Now check your work. With the power cord unplugged, insert a lamp plug into a receptacle. Plug the power cord into a power source. Flip the power switch (the inside toggle) "on" and "off" to see if the light responds properly. Unplug the beam's cord and repeat this procedure for all the receptacles. Now (with the power cord *disconnected!*) connect the shop light to the end of the 8-foot light cord, again plug the power cord in, and check the light switch (the toggle at the beam's end) in the "on" and "off" positions.

Assuming everything works properly, you are now ready to assemble the beam proper (the brace will be assembled later). Remove the mounting screws from the switch and receptacles; they will not be used. Carefully push each unit through its respective hole and center it on the other side. Mark hole locations, drill starter holes, and mount the units with 8-gauge ¾-inch wood screws.

Fig. 1-28. Beam cutouts.

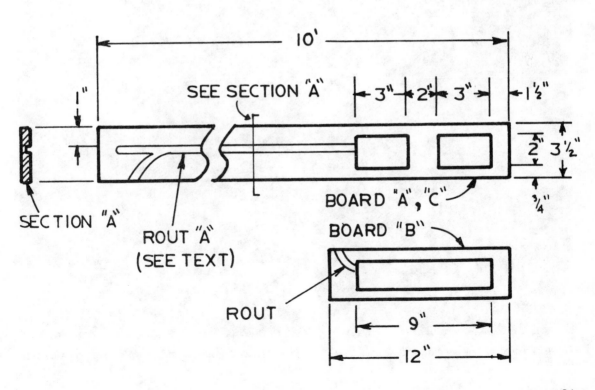

Fig. 1-29. Force the power cord into the smaller routed trough using a lumber scrap. Note the wide trough curve for easy placement.

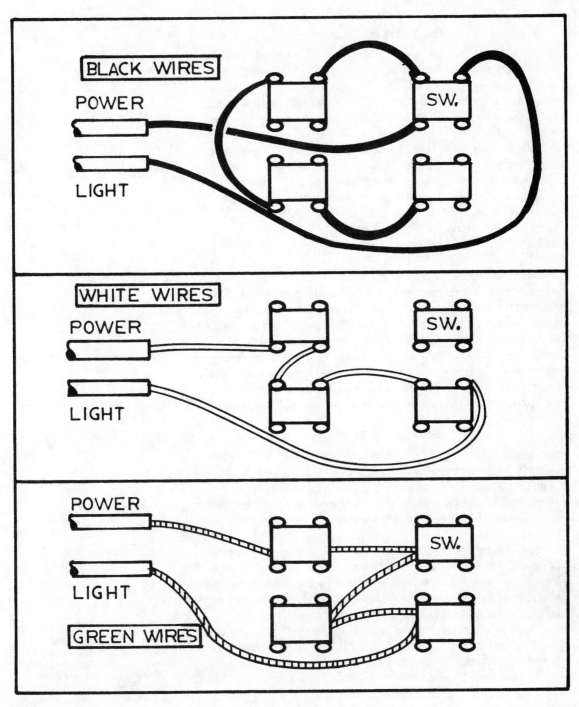

Fig. 1-30. Wiring.

These screws will allow easy removal of the receptacles in the unlikely event of future problems.

Assembling the Beam

The next step is to close and glue the beam. First bend the stiff connecting wires in such a way that they provide a low profile. Then push the pieces together, slowly, until you see each has "found a home" in the narrow void of piece B. Put the light cord into its curved slot in piece B. Make sure once more that the power cord is properly seated.

After making sure pieces A and C remain parallel through their length, apply glue to both sides of piece B and clamp the assembly together tightly. Allow the glue to dry overnight, then remove the clamps. Lay the beam assembly on its side on the floor or another flat surface, board A side down. You might want to put it on a slightly raised surface where the switch toggles can "hang over." This eliminates the chance for building a very slight bow into the finished unit.

Make sure the triangle formed by the brace is truly square. Assemble it with the beam in a "dry run" without nails and glue, following the layout shown in Fig. 1-26. Then "unbuild" this assembly and reconstruct it with glue between the pieces. Check the angle once more; then drive four finish nails through each end of the G brace and its sandwich partners (FGD and CGA) and at the corner formed by CEA. Set the nails ⅛ of an inch below the surface. Turn the assembly over and nail the same areas on the other side. Put wood putty into all the exposed nail holes and sand them smooth.

Mounting the Beam

Position the hinges 4 inches from the top and bottom of the brace assembly (as shown in Fig. 1-26 and Fig. 1-31). To make sure they are lined up properly, fold the free wing down against the edge of the assembly and hold snugly against it while marking or drilling the holes (be sure the countersunk holes are on top, and the pins are in the "up" location).

Mount piece I on the 2×4 (J) as shown in Fig. 1-26, after having cut upright J to the required length as determined by your own shop's dimensions. You can elect to cut piece I so it covers J from top to floor; this is not allowed for in the bill of materials (Fig. 1-26). Lay assembly I J on a flat surface next to the beam assembly and screw the hinges to it (after making sure they are parallel) by inserting ½-inch spacers at both ends. See Fig. 1-31. Drill holes through J to allow the mounting bolts to slip in freely.

The completed assembly must be bolted to a stud within the wall. Hold the upright portion perpendicular against the stud while a helper holds the beam next to the wall. Use a level on the beam to

Fig. 1-31. Use spacers, top and bottom, to ensure squareness of beam to support. Note the position of the exiting cord. If you assemble with the brace pointed downward due to a low ceiling, the cord should exit on the other side.

ascertain when it is level. Drill starter holes into the stud—through the holes already drilled through the upright—and insert and tighten the bolts.

Assembling the Light Carriage

A feature of this light and power beam is the traveling light carriage. Like the rest of the unit, it is actually very easy to construct.

The base for the carriage is a piece of ⅜-inch-thick plywood (see Figs. 1-32A and 1-32B). A router was used to inset the door rollers in order to allow ample clearance of their screws. Assemble the carriage as shown. Then drop it into place in the beam from above. Put S-hooks into the holes for the light's chains, and screw a screw eye into the carriage end that will be nearest the beam's switch end. Insert the free end of the 8-foot light cord downward through the eye.

Your shop light already has a short cord on it. Remove the light tubes, open the wiring assembly, and note the wiring scheme of the

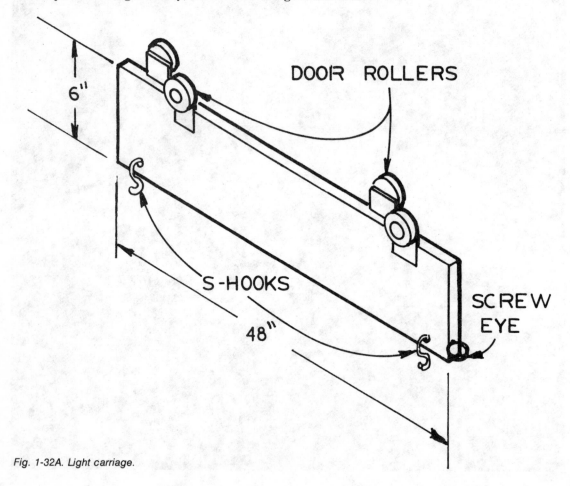

Fig. 1-32A. Light carriage.

Fig. 1-32B. Sliding door rollers are set flush with the surface of 1/3-inch plywood carriage in order to allow ample beam clearance.

three cord wires. Remove the old cord and insert the new one in its place. Making sure the bare wires are insulated, close the assembly and reinsert the tubes. Put S-hooks into the two places provided on the unit's top, attach chains to each (their lengths depend upon your preference), and tighten both legs of these S-hooks with a pair of pliers. Hang the other ends of the chains on the carriage S-hooks. You can now adjust the height above your various work surfaces by simply changing chain links on the carriage hooks.

You've just completed a very important part of your workshop. When a particular job demands that there be light or power. you can now provide it—when and where it is needed.

PROJECT 3: INSULATED WORKSHOP DOORS

A big problem with converting a cold, drafty garage to a workshop is that it often becomes a cold, drafty workshop. Certainly you will want to keep the large door opening, if possible, because some projects almost demand it. But temperatures do get cold . . .

One solution is to build a set of insulated workshop doors. See Tables 1-7 and 1-8. Foam/plywood construction materials stop heat transfer almost as well as insulated walls do, and careful attention to the stops and other trim eliminates drafts. It also has strength to

Table 1-7. Project 3 Tools.

Saw
Hammer
Screwdriver
Square
Countersink Bit
Drill
Adjustable Wrench
Measuring Tape
Pliers

Table 1-8. Project 3 Bill of Materials.

Material	Quantity
2″ × 4″ × 8′ studs	7
⅜″ AC plywood, 4′ × 8′	4
⅝″ foam insulation panels, 4′ × 8′	4
1″ × 4″ × 8′ pine (hinge & upright boards)	5
1″ × 4″ × 12′ pine (cross members)	2
1″ × 2″ × 8′ pine (for stops)	3
4″ brass hinges with screws	6
Bar holders	4
¼″ × 1½″ lag screws (for bar holders)	12
White glue	As needed
8d nails	As needed
6d finish nails	As needed
Weather stripping	24 feet

withstand unauthorized entry. This should certainly be a consideration if you now have or hope to acquire expensive equipment.

A top criterion of this project is attractiveness. The doors described in this section were originally designed for the carriage house of a large Victorian home. A facade popular with turn-of-the-century stables and carriage houses was used. And although it is a two-door package, therefore easy to open and close, passersby will swear it is one piece.

Constructing the Door

The first step is to measure the door opening of your building. Use a level to make sure the sides and top are still plumb; age and perhaps carelessness by the original builder could have taken their toll. Some older buildings might not have finished jambs. This will provide you with an opportunity to make things right. The top casing should allow a half inch of the header to show. The rest of this description assumes that the opening is plumb.

Determine the height of your doors by deducting 1 inch from the opening height. The widths are determined by deducting 1½ inches from the opening's width and dividing the remainder by two. The top, middle, and bottom spaces will be partially or totally covered later by the front trim, and the top and side spaces will be blocked by insulated inside door stops.

The framework of each door is made up of five 2×4s, using half-lap and lapped dado joints, to fit as shown in Fig. 1-33. Cut pieces A, B, C, D and E to the length just determined from your opening measurements. Cut the two pieces of ⅜-inch plywood (F and G) to the same dimensions.

To assemble each door, lay framework pieces A and B on a smooth, flat surface, with lapped areas facing up, and position the three cross pieces C, D and E as shown in Fig. 1-34. Lay plywood F

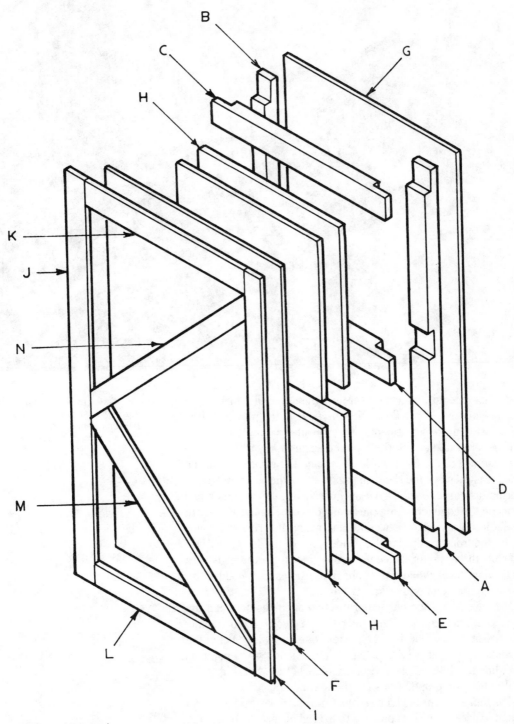

Fig. 1-33. Door framework.

on top (best side up). Now move around the assembly; make sure the framework pieces are flush with the edge of the plywood. It is much easier to make adjustments now than after nailing and gluing.

If you are satisfied, lift the plywood up and apply white glue to the top surface of the framework pieces and between them in the lapped areas. Replace the sheet and again adjust the assembly for an as-perfect-as-possible fit. Drive an 8d nail into each corner and midway on the edge (checking the fit as you go). Then drive four to six nails into each edge between these nails; the trim will cover them on the front except for the inside edge of the left door. Use finish nails there and for the center cross pieces. Set the nails ⅛ of an inch below the plywood surface and fill the holes with wood putty. Now turn the assembly over on its "back."

Measure the inside of each of the two openings between the now-exposed framework pieces, and cut foam pieces (H) to fit using a sharp razor blade. Two stacked pieces completely fill each of the two voids. Now, put a bead of glue along each 2×4 member as before, line up plywood piece G, and nail as before. See Fig. 1-35. Complete the same operations for the second door.

The hinge side of the trim (I) must now be measured, cut, and attached to each door. This piece is to extend beyond the door, top

Fig. 1-34. Lay out the framework. Then check positioning with plywood surface. Apply glue, replace plywood, and nail.

and bottom. The top should overlap the exposed edge of the header after installation (see Fig. 1-36) to leave only a quarter inch of space between it and the top casing of the building. The bottom should extend down past the door's bottom edge to within one quarter inch of the floor or ground surface. On some buildings, there is an incline approach to the garage so it might extend down past the actual floor surface. To determine the exact length and positioning of these boards, it is wise to place the assembly in position in the opening in a "dry run." Place on the ¾-inch space and wedge as later described in the following section.

Put glue on the board, and align it flush with the outside edge of the door. Check the clearances, top and bottom, and then nail firmly with 8d nails. Make sure to avoid the three hinge-joining areas.

To find the hinge hole positions, lay the door on a flat surface again and place the opened hinge 6 inches down from the top of the hinge board. Bend the free wing down against the door's 2×4 edge board to form an approximate 90-degree angle with the other wing. Be sure the hinge side with the countersunk holes is facing up. Then hold the hinge snug against the door and, with a pencil or a long-tipped, ball-point pen, circle each of the hole positions on the 1×4. Mark the center and bottom hinge screw positions in a like manner.

Drill starter holes smaller than the screws supplied with the

Fig. 1-35. After one surface has been glued and nailed to the framework, turn the assembly over and insert a double layer of foam insulation. Then attach the other plywood panel.

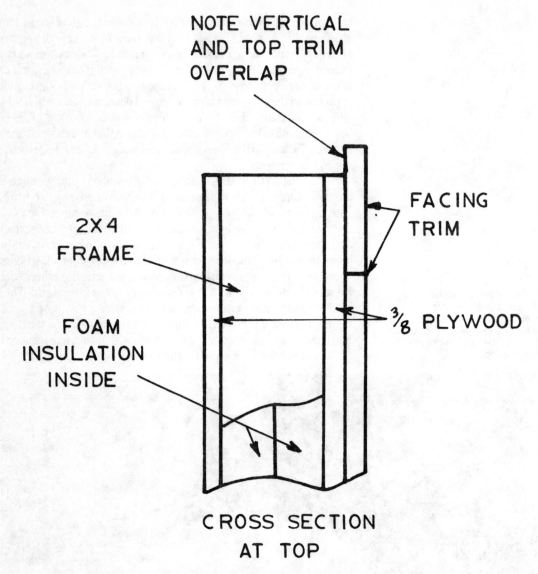

NOTE VERTICAL
AND TOP TRIM
OVERLAP

2X4
FRAME

FACING
TRIM

FOAM
INSULATION
INSIDE

$\frac{3}{8}$ PLYWOOD

CROSS SECTION
AT TOP

hinges. A drill alignment device will help assure straight screws, but it is not absolutely necessary. Attach the hinges making sure they are oriented so their pins fit from the top. If you use an electric drill with a screwdriver bit to drive your screws, be sure to do so carefully; too much torque can easily twist off brass screw heads (making the screws virtually impossible to remove later). Now, attach the hinge board and hinges on the other door.

Note that the center upright trim J, which is the same length as the hinge boards, is attached to only the right-hand door, and that its outside edge extends beyond the door edge by 1 inch. This will cover the planned half-inch gap between the doors, and cover the

Fig. 1-36. The hinge side of the trim.

results of slight adjustments during installation. Although you could put the rest of the trim on now, it is advisable to wait until the doors are hung. This will assure the tightest fit possible. It will also provide comfort inside and the "one big door" look you want on the outside.

Hanging the Doors

Hang the left door first. Place a scrap piece of 1×4 (actually ¾ of an inch thick) on the floor in the opening, within a foot of the left wall, and set the door in position on it (see Fig. 1-37) a half inch from the

Fig. 1-37. A wedge between door and garage floor, made from scrap lumber, aids in leveling the doors. Use a carpenter's level on the edge to ensure a proper fit.

side casing. The top of the hinge board should rest against the edge of the header board. Now, place a wedge under the other corner of the door and adjust it until the door is level (as determined by a level held on the right vertical edge). Again check the hinge-side spacing, top and bottom. Mark and drill the hinge screw holes, screw the hinges solidly into place, and then open the door and remove the scrap wood and wedge. Set the right-hand door into position; repeat the basic process.

Attach the top and bottom trim pieces (K and L) of the right-hand door after measuring them against the door itself and cutting to size. Measure and cut the left-hand door horizontal trim pieces in a similar manner with the door closed. Make sure to allow at least 3/16 of an inch between their right ends and the vertical center trim, piece J, of the right-hand door. There must be enough room to allow clearance for door openings and seasonal contraction and expansion. Yet it must also be close enough to maintain the "one-door" look.

Cutting the "X" members of the trim properly will require some thought and time, but the effort will be amply rewarded in a professional-looking facade. First, take a 1-×-4 board that is long enough to span across opposite corners (see Figs. 1-38 and 1-39) and hold it until its top edge crosses at the top left corner intersection of the left door trim and its bottom edge does the same at the right corner of the right door. Lightly tap in small nails in the door casings—not the trim being measured—and rest the trim on them.

With your hands now free, carefully mark for trim board M, top

Fig. 1-39. Right: Hanging the doors.

Fig. 1-38. This attractive set of shop doors looks like one unit, but it opens in the center to provide easy use. The doors are completely insulated to provide year-round workshop comfort.

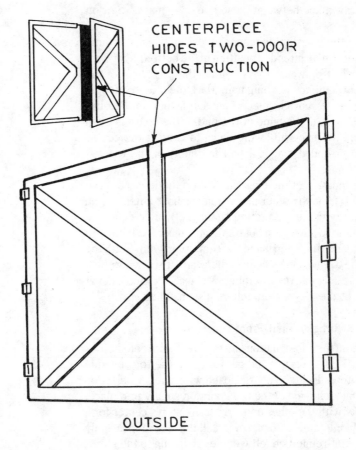

CENTERPIECE
HIDES TWO-DOOR
CONSTRUCTION

OUTSIDE

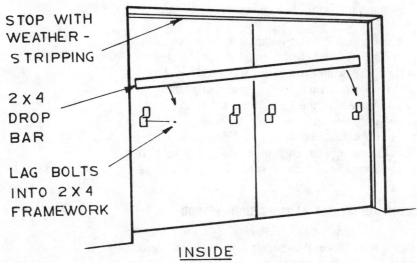

STOP WITH
WEATHER-
STRIPPING

2 X 4
DROP
BAR

LAG BOLTS
INTO 2 X 4
FRAMEWORK

INSIDE

and bottom, where it intercepts the right hinge board I. Remove the trim piece and draw a line between these two edge marks. Saw on that line.

Now replace the board in its diagonal position—but this time with the just-cut end in its intended position in the bottom right door corner—snug against plywood F. As before, the other end of the board should rest on the top aligning nail. Mark the intersection on the inside of the center upright piece J and cut as before. Be sure that the saw kerf is on the outside of the line. If the board is even slightly short, the top end will swing down to contact the center upright, and the extended diagonal will fall short of the top left corner of the left door.

For the continuation of the diagonal line on the left door, you can use the cut left from the other piece. Put the board in the same position as before (with the top resting on the nail), sight down the board in rifle fashion to align with board M, and adjust the trim until there is 3/16 of an inch between it and the center upright J. Mark the intersection at the top and cut as before; then nail into place. Repeat these steps for the second cross member. Make an additional cut at the intersection of the diagonal members just installed.

Airtight, Theft-Proof Finishing

To complete the airtight installation, install weatherproofed stops as shown in Fig. 1-39. Measure and cut to length the top and side pieces of 1-×-2 stops. Hold the doors closed with a heavy object on the outside and tack one end of the top doorstop snugly into place. Then do the same with the other end, adjust the stop's center for a tight fit, and nail completely into place. Install the side stops. Apply vinyl, foam, or metal-reinforced felt weather stripping to the stops, against the closed door, following the manufacturer's installation instructions.

These doors are designed for strength in order to withstand attempts at forced entry. A simple 2-×-4 drop bar, cut just short of the left-stop-to-right-stop width, completes this security. Attach two brackets on the inside of each door, aligned horizontally, as shown in Fig. 1-39. Make sure the lag bolts pass into the doors' center or edge 2-×-4 framework.

This completes the insulated door project. You now have truly beautiful doors that show off your carpentry skills, and you have built-in comfort and security in which to work. It's a good feeling, isn't it?

PROJECT 4: ADJUSTABLE HANGING SHOP MIRROR

The time comes in every craftsman's life when he or she needs a mirror in the shop or work space. Woodworkers need a shop mirror to speed assembly of intricate projects, and to help match grain, texture and other visual qualities for the best results. Artists in many mediums, when working on large table-top projects, need a mirror to get a bird's-eye view, and thus avoid a natural tendency to foreshorten figures. Electronics buffs need a mirror to watch TV screen raster patterns. And if you think through your own projects, you are most likely to see that you could use one to advantage in your workshop.

The large shop mirror shown in Fig. 1-40 was originally designed to eliminate need for a sculptor to make repeated trips up a ladder to get that all-important bird's-eye view of a large horizontal

Fig. 1-40. The mirror can be hung in almost any position using ceiling hooks. In this position, a craftsman at his bench can see the bench surface in a vertical plane in the mirror.

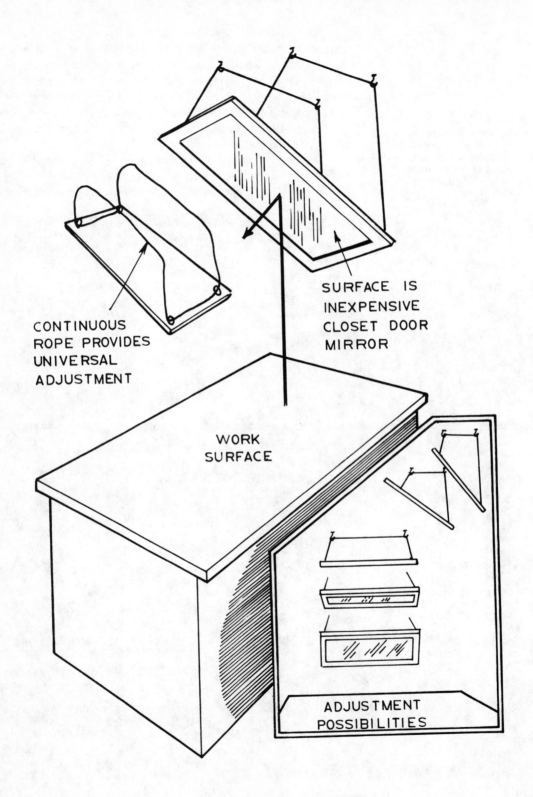

CONTINUOUS
ROPE PROVIDES
UNIVERSAL
ADJUSTMENT

SURFACE IS
INEXPENSIVE
CLOSET DOOR
MIRROR

WORK
SURFACE

ADJUSTMENT
POSSIBILITIES

Table 1-9. Project 4 Tools.

Saw
Hammer
Router
Drill
Adjustable Wrench
Measuring Tape
Pliers

basal relief clay model made for a plaster cast. It has since served many other uses in the shop. Much of its versatility stems from its ultrasimple design. It is large enough to serve almost any need. Because it hangs from the ceiling, it takes up no valuable shop or bench space. Its suspension system makes it almost universally adjustable, and the wide-stance ceiling mounting technique eliminates all chance for unwanted swing and wobble.

Perhaps just as important, it is economical to make. All that is required is a discount-store closet door mirror, ¾-×-2½-inch lumber, clothesline, and miscellaneous machine screws, screw eyes, and hooks. See Table 1-9.

Construction is very simple. First locate the mirror you will use and, if its dimensions differ from those shown in Fig. 1-41 and 1-42, allow for the difference in your own project. If your mirror is an inch *longer* than the one described in Fig. 1-42, add an inch to the length of parts A and B. If it is wider, add to the width of parts C and D.

Assembling the Mirror

After any necessary dimensional changes have been made, cut parts A and B to length. Rabbet a length of ¾-×-2½-inch board (this allows space for kerfs and scrap) as shown in Fig. 1-43. Cut parts F and G from one end; be sure to allow C and D to be their full size after cutting them apart. Next cut parts C and D to size.

Lay parts C and D on a table, parallel to each other, and place the mirror's top and bottom on the rabbeted "shelves" (reflective side up). Then lay parts A and B parallel to each other on the long edges of this assembly—each with one end on a corner of part C and the other end in like position on part D—forming a rectangle. With the edge surfaces flush and the mirror fitting properly, drill *one* hole through each corner. Insert an 8-32 by 2 inch machine screw through from the front (top), and finger-tighten a nut on its end.

With the frame thus loosely assembled, make sure the rectangle is true and drill the second hole in each corner. Insert machine screws as before, screw on their nuts, and tighten all with a screwdriver and wrench or pliers. Glue and nail parts F and G approximately half way between the ends (see Figs. 1-42 and 1-44 for positioning), with the rabbeted portions over the mirror to keep it from moving in the frame. Paint the assembly, and screw the screw eyes into the unit (Fig. 1-45).

Screw the hooks into the ceiling. The actual distances apart aren't crucial except that the "width" distance should be wider than the width of the mirror itself, to eliminate any tendency for it to swing. A "length" distance of 42 inches between front and back hooks is suggested for the mirror because that is the approximate horizontal distance between the top and bottom screw eyes when

Fig. 1-41. Mirror layout.

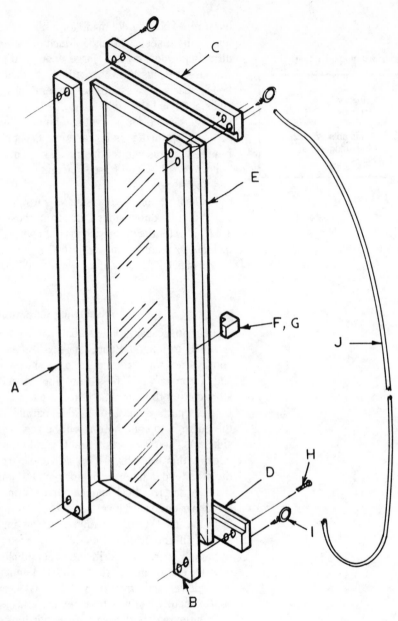

Part	Description	Quantity
A,B	¾″ × 2½″ × 59¾″ lumber	2
C,D	¾″ × 2½″ × 18½″ lumber	2
E	15½″ × 55½″ closet door mirror	1
F,G	¾″ × 1½″ × 2″ lumber	2
H	8-32 × 2″ machine screw and nut	8
I	Screw eyes	4
J	Clothesline	Length needed

Fig. 1-42. Mirror parts and dimensions.

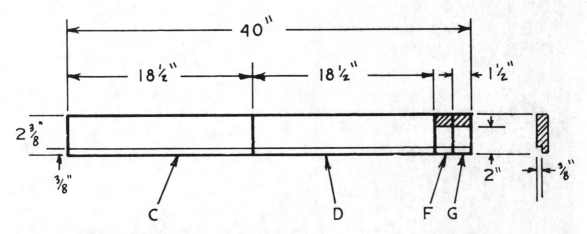

Fig. 1-43. Mirror dimensions.

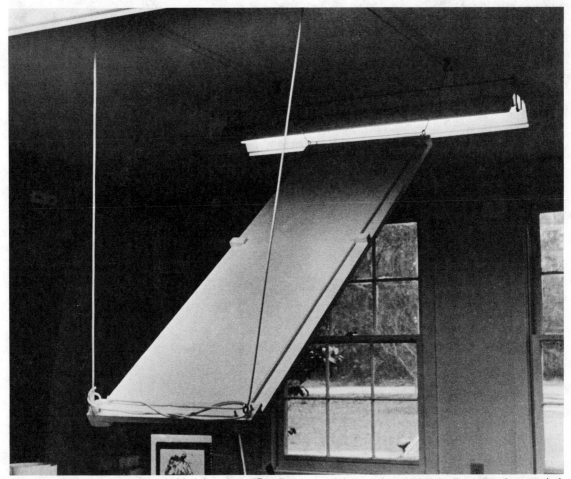

Fig. 1-44. Note the rope position behind the mirror. "Extra" rope was left intact for additional adjustment when needed.

51

the mirror is at a 45-degree angle. That angle provides a vertical
view of work laid flat on a table (Fig. 1-40). Stud location might
affect one of these measurements.

the mirror is at a 45-degree angle. That angle provides a vertical
view of work laid flat on a table (Fig. 1-40). Stud location might
affect one of these measurements.

Fig. 1-45. Details of the rabbet in the bottom piece used to hold the mirror in place. The screweye can be almost any size.

If the mirror height is to remain constant, tie one end to a screw
eye and thread the rope through the others in succession around the
mirror. Then hang the mirror as shown in Figs. 1-40, 1-41, and 1-44.
Hang the mirror at the proper height; then cut the loose end to
length and tie it to the first screw eye.

If you would like to keep the option of adjusting the mirror
height—and there is certainly merit in that—do not cut off the
remaining portion. Coil it instead and tape the coil to the back of the
mirror (out of sight).

Note that in Fig. 1-41 the adjustment possibilities of the mirror
are extensive. The universal nature of the mounting allows it to be
adjusted in every plane in order to provide widely varying views as
required. The mirror can also be easily removed from its supporting
hooks and transported to other sites to provide that helpful look at
the "other side" of your next project.

PROJECT 5: PEGBOARD AND SHELF UNIT

Let's assume you have built the first four projects of this book. Now
you have light to see by, a bench to work on, and a mirror to help you
see your work from the proper perspective. It's time now to provide
a place to hold your tools conveniently when you are not using them.
See Tables 1-10 and 1-11.

Table 1-10. Materials List.

Part	Dimensions	Quantity	Notes
A	1½″ × 3½″ × 92½″ stud	3	See Fig. 1-48
B	1½″ × 3½″ × 10¼″ stud	3	See Fig. 1-48
C	1½″ × 3½″ × 11½″ stud	3	See Fig. 1-48
D	1½″ × 3½″ × 92½″ stud	2	See Fig. 1-3
E	¼″ × 4′ × 8′ pegboard	1*	
F	¾″ × 9¼″ 8′ pine	1	
G	¾″ × 3½″ × 8′ pine	1	
H	Six-receptacle box	1	

*Two needed if bottom storage is desired

The combination pegboard and shelf unit shown in Fig. 1-46 will do the job admirably. Because its large upper surface is pegboard, you can use easily available hooks to make any tool arrangement you want. You can change that arrangement later when you acquire more tools or if you simply believe another arrangement will work better.

The built-in shelf provides an equally useful function. Many home craftsmen have discovered the space-saving, clutter-repellent qualities of plastic drawer cabinets for screws, nails, small tools, and miscellaneous items. But they often keep them on the workbench and that takes up valuable work space.

The long and deep shelf in this unit lifts things up and out of the way, yet keeps them within handy reach. It also provides ample room for such items as catalogs and other reference books, a telephone extension, a radio, or virtually any other item you'd like to have close at hand.

But that's not all. By putting a pegboard beneath the shelf, you can double your tool storage and display area. Indeed, if you are using a portable workbench, you can use this storage area even as the bench is located under the shelf. The overhang of the benchtop in Project 1 will allow storage of deep items even when it is pushed all the way in. If you want to store even deeper items there, it is a simple matter to put 2×4 spacers at the worktop level, and thus gain even more depth.

If you have a stationary workbench, consider setting it 3 feet or more away from this pegboard wall, and work from a position between them. Or put it on one wall at a corner and install this pegboard unit on the adjacent wall. Obviously, if your layout demands that you use a stationary bench in front of this unit, you can eliminate the lower pegboard and save money.

An additional feature is the unit's portability. The unit is so constructed that it can be held to the wall with only a few nails. When you want to use that room for another purpose, simply pull the nails and remove it. Along with the moveable workbench, this unit

Table 1-11. Project 5 Tools.

Saw
Hammer
Square
Scroll Saw
Measuring Tape

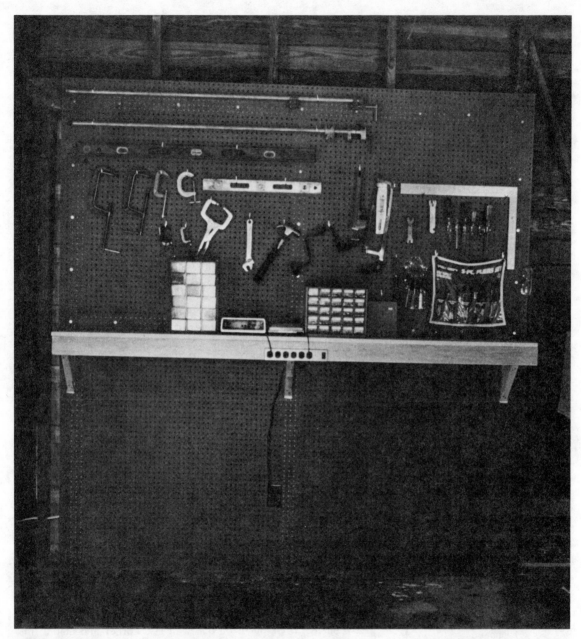

helps keep you flexible to make changes as needs and preferences arise.

Assemble the Unit

Start by selecting five straight pre-cut studs or cut your own to 92½-inch lengths. Now, cut the proper lap areas as shown in Figs. 1-47 and 1-48. Notice that the three part As (the uprights) have

Fig. 1-46. This pegboard and shelf unit provides the utmost in tool-storage flexibility. Note the large area beneath the shelf that is ideal for storage of many tools and accessories.

54

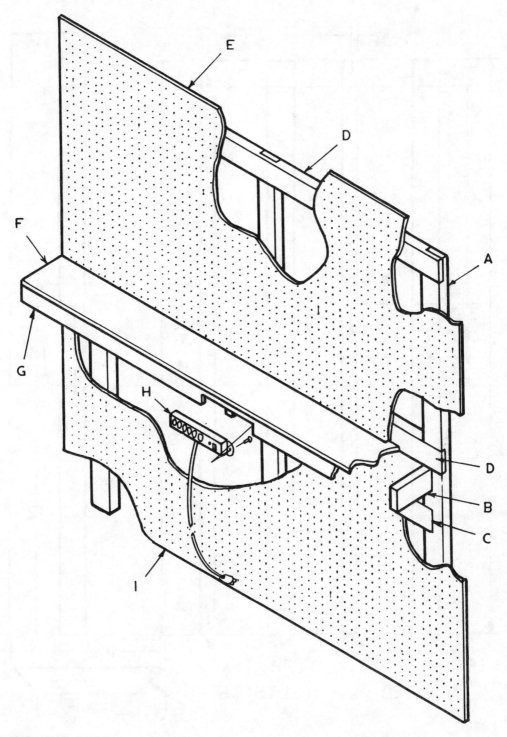

Fig. 1-47. Assembly details.

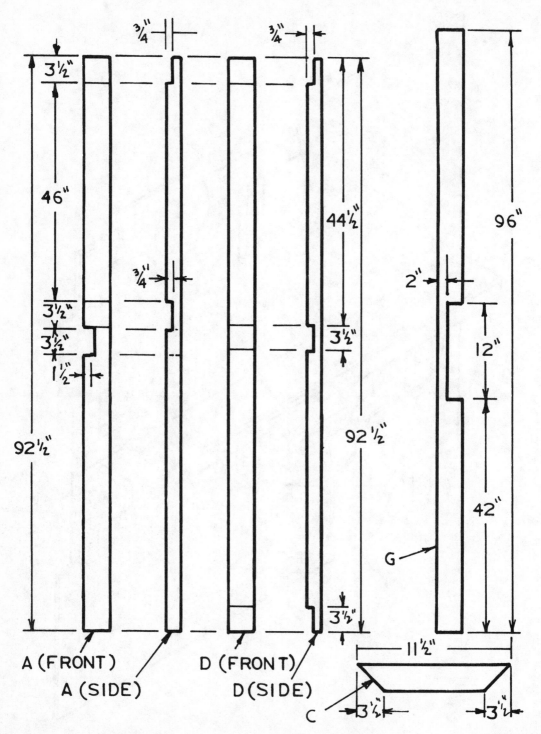

Fig. 1-48. Component dimensions.

center cuts from two planes of the board. One, ¾-inch deep, allows part D to set into it so that the top surfaces are flush. The other, cut out of the side of the stud, just under the first cut is 1½-inches deep.

Make three A-B-C assemblies as shown in Fig. 1-49. Place one end of B into the side cut of A so that B's end is even with the back edge of A; nail it into place with one nail. Place part C under it as a brace, with one angled end flush with the bottom of part B, and the other flush with the front surface of part A; nail it to both members. Check first to make sure B is perpendicular to A, and then drive another nail through B and A. Use this first unit as a pattern for the other two A-B-C uprights.

Lay these three subassemblies on the floor, with the protruding ends of parts B facing upward, and with the A parts parallel to each other and about 4 feet apart. Now, lay the two parts D across them—one at the top, mating with the top lap cuts, the other across the middle, mating with the lap cuts just above parts B—and drive one nail into each of the six junctions (Fig. 1-50). Use a square to make sure the A's are perpendicular with the D's; then drive a second nail through each junction.

The shelf is next. Center F on the three support parts B (see Fig. 1-47) with the inside edge against part D, and nail it into place. Notice that the other edge extends beyond the ends of parts B. Nail receptacle box H to the back side of piece G. Then lay part G into this area under the shelf's outer edge, with its own ends flush with the ends of the shelf. Nail G to the two end parts B, and drive additional nails down through the edge of F into the edge of G. Notice that the center B part provides a support against the outlet box (Fig. 1-51) holding it in place when plugs are pushed into it.

Fig. 1-49. The first assembly step is to make three A-B-C braces. Make sure the tops are level.

Fig. 1-50. Lay A-B-C assemblies on the floor, and connect them with the specially cut cross pieces. Install the shelf top before attaching the pegboard.

Fig. 1-51. Nail the receptacle box to the inside of part G before installing the latter. Drive nails down through shelf into part G. Note that the A-B-C assembly provides a firm support for the receptacles.

Stand the unit up against its selected spot on the wall and attach it with three or four nails. It will not take many nails because most of the weight is transferred to the floor via the A pieces. Now attach pegboard E. Center it, left and right, on the A-D framework with its bottom edge resting on shelf F. Although you could use spacers between the pegboard and the framework to allow use of pegboard hooks over the framework, you'll find in practice that you can fill the pegboard with tools without using those areas. Simply drive roofing nails through pegboard holes into the framework to hold the pegboard in place. If you ever want to move the backboard unit, it will be

Fig. 1-52. Nail cleats to A-B-C assembly in order to provide support for the bottom pegboard.

easy enough to remove them and the pegboard before separating the framework from the wall.

As a final step, add the bottom pegboard. Attach small cleats next to the A-B-C assemblies where needed in order to provide support for the pegboard edge (Fig. 1-52). A receptacle was built into this unit to provide power for outlet box H.

Experiment with Tool Layout

Now comes the moment you have been waiting for. Gather all of your tools and lay them on a 4- ×-8-foot area of the floor as you sort them into a logical pattern. Think in terms of how frequently you will use the tools. Infrequently used items such as circular saw blades and glue clamps might go at the top, while screwdrivers and similar high-use items would logically be just above the shelf within easy reach. Remember to allow room on this floor "pattern" for your utility drawer sets.

When you are satisfied with the basic layout, put hooks into the pegboard and transfer the tools from the floor to a like position on the board. Remember, of course, that you can change this layout at any time. Now put your utility drawer boxes into place, plug in your radio, and you're done.

2

Storage

PROPER STORAGE—OR THE LACK OF IT—CAN MAKE OR BREAK a home craftsman. It takes a strong-willed person indeed to continue working in the midst of chaos, and there is an even chance that the results of that work will be second rate. If you can't find your tools and materials when you need them, and if they are constantly in the way when you *don't* need them, it is a small wonder that frustration overtakes creation and we slink back to our easy chairs to consider less aggravating energy outlets.

This section is based loosely on grandmother's admonition that there should be a place for everything and everything should be in its place. Presented are several projects designed to provide a home for almost everything used in the shop. With these projects, lumber hangs on walls, too-good-to-discard scrap stacks neatly on end, and electric tools stay at home until needed (then are instantly ready to work). A drawing cabinet keeps all of your instruments hidden from flying sawdust, yet makes them readily accessible when they are needed. Perhaps the most interesting project of all is the rolling panel saw and storage unit. It takes 4-×-8-foot panels to the job, saws them for you, and then glides effortlessly back to its assigned spot by the wall.

If you make all of these projects, and follow grandmother's advice, you'll have room to work and everything will be accessible to you in the bargain. That's not a bad situation!

PROJECT 6: PANEL SAW AND STORAGE UNIT

Nothing is quite as difficult as single-handedly sawing 4-×-8 panel with a radial-arm saw or circular saw. Using sawhorses and a portable saw sometimes works better, but cutting accuracy can suffer. If you do a lot of work with plywood and other panel material, you're sure to reach your frustration level soon.

The 7-foot, 3-inch high panel saw shown in Fig. 2-1 will make that cutting chore a pleasure. Primary, of course, is the fact that it cuts panels—up to ¾ of an inch thick and 4×8 feet long and wide—

Fig. 2-1. This panel saw and rack, easily built by the home handyman, handles panels up to 3/4 of an inch thick and 4 × 8 feet in width and length. It easily rolls out of the way between jobs.

Fig. 2-2. Cross cutting is accomplished simply by putting the saw down through the panel.

with ease. The operator simply puts the panel into place and pulls the saw down through it in a "climbing" cut (Fig. 2-2) or locks the carriage in place and pulls panels through for panel-length cuts (Fig. 2-3). You will find yourself using this saw for many cutting jobs you might normally do with another saw.

There are other bonuses. For one, it is also a panel storage unit. Full-size and large pieces of panels are stored neatly on the bottom shelf, and smaller pieces are kept on the upper one (Fig. 2-4). The whole assembly—saw, panels and all—rolls out for use wherever you want it in the shop, and then glides effortlessly back to its out-of-the-way home between jobs. The one pictured is kept in front of wall-mounted lumber storage racks, making double use of the wall area.

Another very important feature is the built-in cutting and drawing guide. A 4-foot steel ruler mounted on the saw carriage track's right vertical member provides a true perpendicular to a panel resting in position on the 2-×-4 panel support beam (Fig. 2-5). That means it can be used as a guide to draw cutting marks directly on a panel or to draw on a piece of paper thumbtacked to a board. For horizontal lines, you can either use an artist's triangle against the straightedge or mount a horizontal rule on the moving saw carriage.

By using a panel with an attached horizontal "fence" on which to rest pieces of cardboard, matt board, paper, and other cuttable materials, you can use a razor knife to quickly cut them to size. By lining up a carriage-mounted pointer with a selected measurement on the rule, you can automatically set the saw position for ripping panels. Panels can also be measured against a backboard-mounted metal rule for on-the-spot cutting.

Fig. 2-3. Turn the saw carriage sideways for ripping, and hold in position with a small C-clamp at the top and bottom on the left rail.

Fig. 2-4. Right: The back of the portable unit has a storage area for full panels at the bottom and small pieces on the shelf at the top. Notice that the weights counterbalance the saw carriage.

The Frame

If you follow these step-by-step directions, the panel saw and storage unit is relatively easy to build. Construction is done with subassemblies to give you as many opportunities as possible to check your work. See Tables 2-1, 2-2, and 2-3.

Start first with the side assemblies, made up of parts A, D, and E (right assembly as viewed from the sawing position) and B, C, and F (left assembly), as identified in Fig. 2-6. First cut parts A and B according to Fig. 2-7 and place one on top of the other, to make sure their dimensions are identical. Note that the lap-joint cutouts on opposite sides of the boards are slightly wider than 2×4's actual width to allow for a slight "leaning" of upright parts C and D. At part A and B ends opposite the "lap" cutouts, mark a line across the top, 9½ inches from the end (see Fig. 2-7). Use a square to ensure accuracy.

Lay part B on a flat surface with the lap cut up and on the left end. Cut part C to length, cut out the "lap" at the end, and lay part C perpendicular to B, with the lap portions mated. Now lay part F across B and C so that its top right corner is flush with the top right corner of C, and its right edge near the other end is even with the line previously drawn on part B. Drive a small nail through the upper right corner of F and C (Fig. 2-8).

Fig. 2-5. Built-in steel horizontal and vertical rules allow easy measurement of stock.

Table 2-1. Project 6 Tools.

Saw
Hammer
Screwdriver
Square
Countersink Bit
Router
Drill
Scroll Saw
Clamps
Adjustable Wrench
Measuring Tape
Pliers

Table 2-2. Fasteners.

Fasteners

F-1	¼″ × 2″ carriage bolt (with nut)	4
F-2	¼″ × 1½″ carriage bolt (with wing nut)	2
F-3	¼″ × 1¼″ lag bolt	16
F-4	¼″ × 2½″ lag bolt	9
F-5	¼″ × 3″ lag bolt	12
F-6	8 × ¾″ wood screw	37
F-7	10 × 1¼″ wood screw	4
F-8	10 × 1½″ wood screw	18
F-9	U-bolts	2

Note: Use washers under nuts of all carriage bolts and under heads of all lag bolts. See Figs. 2-6 and 2-7.

Table 2-3. Panel Saw Frame Materials List.

Note: Wood required for the following includes lodge pole studs, five 8-foot pieces of ¾″ × 3½″ C grade fir, one 12-foot piece of ¾″ × 1½″ C grade fir, and one 4′ × 8′ BB or AC ¾″ plywood. Select each piece carefully for straightness and appearance.

A	1½″ × 3½″ × 30″	⎫
B	1½″ × 3½″ × 30″	⎬ see Fig. 2-7
C	1½″ × 3½″ × 82″	⎪
D	1½″ × 3½″ × 82″	⎭
E	¾″ × 3½″ × 82″	
F	¾″ × 3½″ × 82″	
G	1½″ × 3½″ × 48″	
H	1½″ × 3½″ × 48″	
I	¾″ × 1½″ × 11″	
J	¾″ × 1½″ × 11″	
K	1½″ × 3½″ × 79⅜″	
L	¾″ × 3½″ × 48″ (3 pieces)	
M	¾″ × 3½″ × 14″ (2 pieces)	
N	¾″ × 3½″ × 3½″ (2 pieces)	
O	¾″ × 3½″ × 45″ (2 pieces)	
P	¾″ × 1½″ × 45″	
Q	¾″ × 1½″ × 48″	
R	1½″ × 3½″ × 48″ see Fig. 2-7	
S	¾″ × 48″ × 79⅜″ BB or AC plywood	
T	1½″ × 3½″ × 8″	
U	⅝″ × 4′ bolt	
V	Pulley, ⅝″ bore, 2½″ diameter	
W	Nylon clothesline (10 feet)	
X	Weight(s)	
Y	Metal rule, 36″	
Z	Wheels	

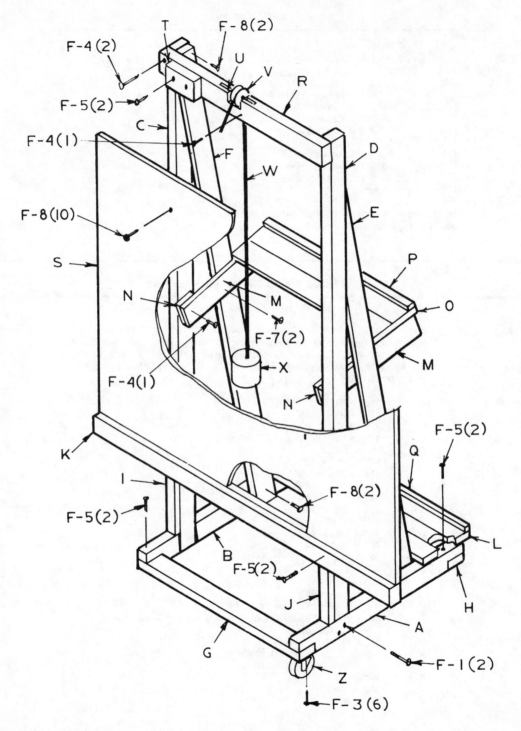

Fig. 2-6. Assembly details.

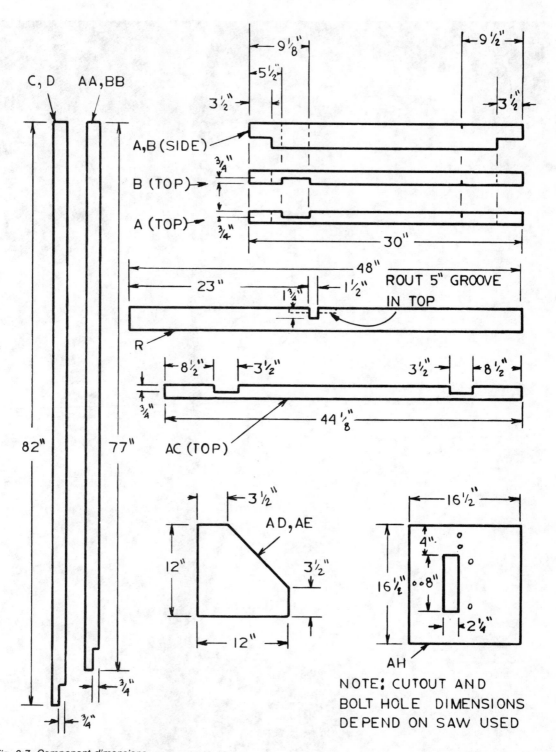

Fig. 2-7. Component dimensions.

Fig. 2-9. Correct position of parts A, D, and E. Part D is a 2 × 4 that is cut to leave a flush surface when mated with part A.

Adjust the bottom of part C so that its left corner touches the left "wall" of the lap cut in part B, and its right corner is flush with the bottom surface of part B (Fig. 2-9). Adjust part F similarly, so that the right edge is still lined up with the pencil mark on the top of B, and its bottom left corner is flush with the bottom edge of B. Check both C and F positions once again, and then drive two nails into each junction to maintain them.

Assemble the other side (parts A, D, and E) in the same manner, so that it is a mirror image of the first assembly. Then lay one assembly on the other to make sure they are identical in shape. Correct any problems now so that the final project will not be out of alignment.

Lay parts G and H parallel on the floor, and set the two completed side assemblies on them. Temporarily nail a scrap piece of lumber across the top of the two side assemblies (two nails at each end for stability) so that they are 48 inches apart (outside edge to outside edge). Check alignment of all parts carefully. Drill holes and insert the bolts and screws that are to hold the frame together (Fig. 2-10).

Now prepare cross member R as shown in Fig. 2-7. It is important that the *groove* of the pulley, that will later fit here, is centered. Some pulleys, such as the one used here, have a collar on one side that holds a set screw, and this collar must be allowed for when making the cutout. The pulley is not to be tightened in this application; be sure it will turn on the axle you select. After making

Fig. 2-8. Left: A single nail temporarily holds parts D and E in position, screws will later secure them permanently.

Fig. 2-10. Assembly A-D-E is bolted to cross pieces G and H. Screws and bolts have already been put into place and part J has been attached.

the cutout and routing out a groove in the top edge of cross member R to receive the pulley axle, position the piece at the top of the side assemblies, drill the appropriate holes, and tighten in the lag bolts.

Because the position of part K is crucial to accurate cutting and time and heavy use could possibly force it out of alignment, supports I and J are next nailed into place. Be sure that they are of exact length, and that they rest on A and B in order to transfer backboard and panel weight to the base. Then lay K across their tops, check alignments once more, drill the necessary holes through K, and screw in the lag bolts.

Now nail the floor (parts L) across A and B, where stored panels will be, to extend from the end of parts A and B back to the front edges of E and F. Lengths of ¾-×-3½-inch boards were used for the unit pictured, but you may elect to use a piece of plywood or other panel material.

The upper shelf supports are next. Cut M and N to length, and nail them together as shown in Fig. 2-6. Make two such assemblies and place them in T-square fashion on part F (and E). Slide each assembly up until the bottom edge is 49 inches from the panel support floor (L), as measured along the outside edge of F (and E). This will allow 1-inch clearance for full-size panels resting on that surface of E and F. Put two lengths of ¾-×-3½-inch board across these supports for a shelf (or use plywood or other material), and nail board P and Q to the shelf and floor edges to serve as stored-material retainers (Fig. 2-11).

The backboard (Fig. 2-12) is next. Note that this is the remainder of a 4-×-8 piece of ¾-inch plywood, after a full 16½-inch width has been cut off for the carriage and guide gussets (described later). Center it on part K, and draw vertical lines that line up with the center of parts C and D. Drill five equally spaced holes along each line—with the first and last within 2 inches of the opposite backboard edges—and countersink screws so that their heads are below the backboard surface.

The Saw Guide Assembly

Because the accuracy of the panel cut depends upon the accuracy with which the saw guide itself is constructed, make all measurements and cuts as carefully as possible. Select straight 2×4s and be sure joints are square before nailing and gluing.

First cut part AC to the dimensions shown in Fig. 2-13. Cut AA and AB to length, then cut the lap area at the end so that the parts fit snugly into the cutouts in part AC. Lay AC on the floor, cutout side up, put glue into the cutouts and place AA and AB into position. Now put glue on these three parts where they will be covered by gussets

Fig. 2-11. Shelf detail shows correct positioning and fastening. Bolts could be used instead of screws.

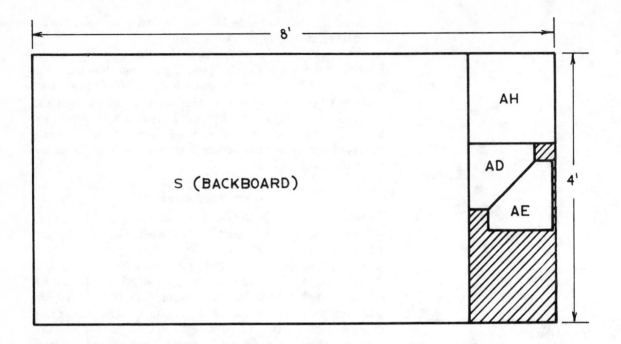

Fig. 2-12. Backboard details.

AD and AE, and lay these pieces into position.

Use a carpenter's square to make sure AA and AB are each absolutely square with AC. Measure between them along their lengths to be sure they are spaced the same distance apart at all points. Constantly check these measurements and angles as you first drive starter nails through the lapped area, and then as you also nail the gussets and AC, AA, and AB.

Lay the assembly on its face. Lay railing AL next to the inside of each upright with its open side facing up (you need 72 inches on each side; you will have to buy four pieces and cut two to fit). With the bottom ends of the rails touching AC, mark oblong screw holes on the upright pieces (through holes in the rails) and drill screw-starting holes in the center of each oblong (Fig. 2-14). Then put a railing in place and insert a screw at each end and—after adjusting the rail so it is flush with the front of the assembly—tighten these screws down. Insert and tighten screws for the rest of the railing. Now glue part AF to AC, midway between AA and AB, to serve as a stop for the saw carriage.

To mount the guide to the frame, center it on part G, between part C and part D. Let it lean back against part K and adjust the position of AC on G until the uprights AA and AB touch both frame parts K and R.

Open the hinges and place each one about 5 inches from A and B, with one wing laying on G and the other leaning back on AC. Mark and drill screw holes and tighten the screws. Do not be concerned

Fig. 2-13. Saw guide assembly.

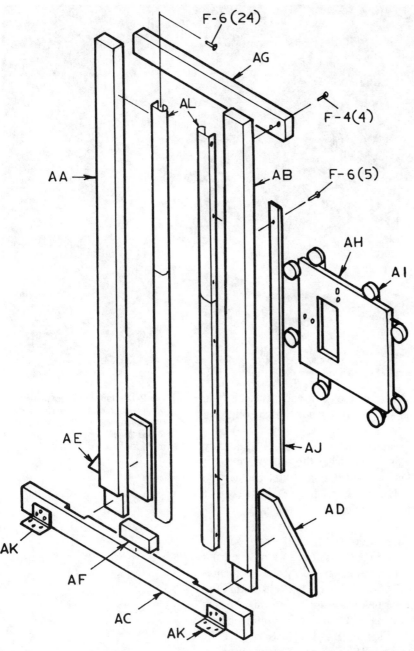

F-6(24)

AG

F-4(4)

AL

AA

AB

F-6(5)

AH

AI

AE

AJ

AK

AD

AF

AC

AK

AA	1½″ × 3½″ × 81″	AG	1½″ × 3½″ 26⅞″
AB	(Same as AA)	AH	¾″ × 16½″ × 16½″ BB or AC plywood
AC	1½″ × 3⅜″ × 44″ (see Fig. 2-7)	AI	National 182 interior sliding door hangers (8)
AD	(Special cut; see Fig. 2-7)	AJ	Four-ft. metal rule
AE	(Special cut; see Fig. 2-7)	AK	Hinges, 4″, brass (2)
AF	1½″ × 2″ × 4½″	AL	1½″ × 3½″ × 77″ (National No. 180 track, two 44″ pieces cut to length)

with the space between the hinges and the guide and the frame. The important thing is to allow the weight of the guide to rest solidly on the frame.

To complete the carriage guide assembly, place AG squarely across AA and AB, so its top edge just touches the bottom edge of R on the main frame, and drill for and insert the lag bolts. The friction between the two will serve to hold the carriage guide in its correct position. One surface can later be sanded, if necessary, to "adjust" this contact point.

Attach the 4-foot-long straightedge, AJ. Drill five mounting holes in the straightedge—close to its "left" edge as viewed from above—with the measurement markings on the right. Use a countersink drill to ream each one from the back (or bottom) so that the screw heads will be flush with or below the surface. Swing the saw guide assembly into contact with parts K and R, and carefully mark, on the right upright AB, where it is intersected by the top edge of K. Rout out a recess for the straightedge so that when mounted its bottom surface will be flush with the bottom surface of the upright. Mount the straightedge so its measurements can be easily seen (with its bottom end at that line). Be sure the edge is parallel to the upright edge and thus perpendicular to support beam K. The positioning, up and down, should be such that the straightedge can be

Fig. 2-14. Mark screw holes through oblong openings in the rail. Then remove the rail to drill starter holes in the center of the mark. This will allow room for later adjustment.

used as an accurate measuring instrument on panels placed on part K.

The Saw Carriage

The saw carriage is the focal part of the whole panel saw because it carries the saw that will accomplish the work. It is made up of a square piece of plywood, eight sliding door hangers, two U-bolts, and two or more bolts to hold the saw in place.

If you have a 7¼-inch saw you can devote exclusively to this service, you can attach it permanently. Cross-cutting is accomplished by effortlessly gliding the carriage up and down; it is counterbalanced by a weight (X) hidden within the panel saw frame, behind the backboard. If you want to rip the length of a panel, simply unsnap the counterbalance weight and momentarily hook the snap onto a lag bolt screwed into piece R for that purpose. Push the carriage off the upper end of the tracks, turn it 90 degrees and re-insert it, this time using the other four rollers. Snap the counterbalance weight rope back in place, lock the carriage by tightening a small C-clamp onto the railing above and below the carriage, and then feed the panel through, from left to right (Fig. 2-15).

To make the carriage, first cut the carriage board; make sure it is a full 16½ inches square. In other words, the saw kerf should be outside this dimension.

Place the selected saw on this board so that the bottom—the part that normally slides on the wood while cutting—is centered in both directions. Use a square to make a side edge of the bottom, and thus the blade, is parallel to the edge of the carriage board. Now mark and drill the bolt holes in the board (if there are no holes in the saw bottom, drill them now), and mark the location of the cutout where the saw blade extends downward through the bottom. Saw this total area out of the board in order to prevent the best vision for lining up the blade with a mark on a to-be-cut panel.

With the saw guide assembly lying on its "face" (as before), place the carriage board midway (and parallel) between the uprights AA and AB. Now place two sliding door hangers (AI), on each side, engaged within the track and about 2 inches down (or up) from the corners (see Fig. 2-15). Drill a screw-starting hole in the *middle* of the diagonal opening located in the center of each hanger and insert a screw in each. Do *not* put screws in the other holes at this time. Now, turn the board 90 degrees and attach the other four hangers in a like manner.

Mount the saw by pushing carriage bolts up through the carriage and the saw bottom and by tightening the saw down with wing nuts. Attach U-bolts (put nuts on both sides of the carriage) for eventual counterbalance attachment.

Lean the guide assembly toward you, on its hinges, and insert

Fig. 2-15. Left: The carriage has two sets of hangers in order to allow rotation for cross cutting and ripping. Mark diagonal holes and drill screw starter holes in their center. Yardsticks are used as temporary supports to hold the carriage at correct working height.

the carriage into its rail guides—in its cross-cutting (up and down) position. Lay a straightedge along the blade and measure between each end and a rail (Fig. 2-16). Adjust the carriage position until the blade is parallel to the rail (that is, the two measurements are identical). Adjust the hangers inward toward the carriage center, as much as possible, by sliding the diagonal grooves along the screws until there is no play between carriage and rails. Double-check both parallel positions and tightness as you slide the carriage to different positions. When satisfied, drill for and place one additional screw in each hanger. Now, push the guide up into working position and check for looseness once again along the total length of the saw guide assembly. If all is operational insert the other screws.

Go through these same basic steps with the saw turned in the "rip" position. Use a square rather than measurements to test for squareness.

To make the counterbalance, put the axle bolt through the pulley (see Figs. 2-6 and 2-7). Drop the assembly into the groove and cutout already made in part R so that the pulley groove lines up with the topmost carriage U-bolt. As noted before, the assembly itself may not be centered, depending upon the pulley configuration.

Weigh the carriage board with the saw mounted (the assembly shown weighs 13 pounds), and tie appropriate weights to one end of

Fig. 2-16. Align carriage carefully as you attach the door hangers. First, use only one screw in diagonal slot and then tighten the fit in the rail.

a length of clothesline. Adjust its length so that the carriage can traverse the entire length of the guide with the weights hitting neither the floor nor the upper frame member R. Two sashweights were used on the panel saw shown. Bricks, a paint bucket filled with cement or heavy metal pieces, and any of numerous other home-made weights can be used.

The last step is to mount the wheels. Turn the unit on its back and attach the casters in the extreme corners with the lag bolts. Be sure to put the two casters with brakes on the front so that they can be locked easily when you are preparing to use the saw.

Preparing the Saw for Use

The saw is now ready for testing and use. With the guide laid back in position against parts K and R, adjust the saw so that its blade touches the backboard, and lock it into that position. With the power still off, roll it down the backboard so that it leaves a track. Use a square to see if the track is true. If you want, cut a line in a panel placed on part K—with the saw adjusted so that it doesn't cut all the way through—and test that line. Slight adjustments can still be made by moving the top of the guide assembly one way or the other. When the exact line is found, make part T and bolt it to part R, next to the guide upright. Round its edge so that the guide assembly will easily find its "home" each time it goes to the sawing position.

Raise the saw to its uppermost position, and adjust the blade depth until it will cut a kerf of perhaps 1/16 of an inch. The saw used in the model, outfitted with a 7¼-inch diameter blade, cuts a kerf of just over ⅛ of an inch deep when extended to its full depth. The depth can be varied permanently by adjusting railing AH.

You might want to use a special, thin hollow-ground, panel-cutting blade designed to provide the narrowest possible cuts to save expensive paneling and to assure fine cuts. For production sawing where you are cutting thick plywood for various around-the-home projects, consider using a good carbon-tipped blade for long life and good cuts.

Now, turn the power saw on and pull the saw down slowly (allowing it to make its cut in the backboard). Use a carpenter's square once again to document the kerf's accuracy.

When you are satisfied with the way the saw tracks, it is time to mount the steel rule along the top right of the backboard. Rout out a "shelf" the length, width and depth of the rule just as you did for the previous 4-foot rule and countersink screw holes as before. Then lay the rule in its shelf so that the extreme left end just touches the saw kerf mark. Carefully drill holes through those in the rule (and into the backboard). Tighten down the screws so that they are flush (or below) the rule's surface.

To cross cut a piece of paneling to size, you need only put the stock on the support member K, slide it so that its top right corner is at the required measurement, and move the saw down over the panel.

The panel saw and storage unit is now ready for use. Gather up your panels and pieces, put them in their new home, and look through these pages for that first project requiring panel cuts. Happy cutting!

PROJECT 7: LUMBER AND MATERIALS STORAGE RACK

Builders, do you know where your lumber is?

As you sit there in your easy chair, your expensive lumber might be out in the elements. Or it may be leaned up, forgotten, in an unused corner of the garage or laying haphazardly in the rafters. Undoubtedly, many workshop enthusiasts have long ago lost track of just what lumber they *do* have, and for good reason: many simply do not have good storage available.

The lumber and materials storage rack shown in Fig. 2-17 can solve the problem. It uses your shop rafters (or joists) for its basic support and hangs high, flush against a wall. You'll have ample room underneath it for other storage and projects.

The rack has four support units (Fig. 2-18). The number of support units you'll need depends on how long the storage wall is and on the lengths of lumber you're likely to use. The wall is 17 feet long so four support units are used to provide for 16-foot long pieces

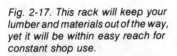
Fig. 2-17. This rack will keep your lumber and materials out of the way, yet it will be within easy reach for constant shop use.

Fig. 2-18. Left: The number of
supports needed depends upon
the size of your storage area and
the amount of materials to be
stored. Figure one unit for every
4 feet of length.

of lumber. You'll need an additional support unit for every 4 feet of length; that is, two units for 8-foot lumber, three for 12-foot, and so on.

Further, each support unit in the rack shown has four braces. You can cut that to three—or increase it to five—depending upon your shop ceiling height and your preferences. By determining the number of lumber layers and support units needed, you've automatically determined the number of 2×4 braces required (the rack shown uses 16 braces). See Tables 2-4 and 2-5.

The Support Units

Use the adjustable fixture described in Project 19 to cut the braces to the proper shape, as shown in Fig. 2-19.

Cut the side pieces A to length from 1-×-6 stock (actually ¾×5½ inches). Lay one of these on a work surface and position one brace B so its lower edge is flush with the bottom of the side piece, and its widest end is flush with the side piece edge. Drive a small finish nail through the extreme top right corner to hold this position and mount the other braces in similar manner at 10-inch intervals (Fig. 2-19).

Move the loose end of each brace piece up an additional half inch (they hinge on their finish nails) to provide a slight upward tilt that will help hold stacked lumber in place. Drive a small nail through each brace, opposite from the finish nail already driven, to maintain its position relative to the side piece on which it rests.

Then position the other side piece A directly over the first one (with the braces located between them), and drive five 8d nails through each side-brace-side assembly. Turn the assembly over and drive four more nails into each brace from that side (Fig. 2-20).

Use this first support unit assembly as a pattern for the other support units. It is important that they match as closely as possible in order that the stored lumber contacts the braces in each.

Hanging the Support Units

The next step is to hang the units. If you have a basement workshop

Table 2-4. Project 7 Tools.

Saw
Hammer
Measuring Tape

Table 2-5. Materials List for a Four-Brace, Four-Support, Three-Shelf Unit.

Material	Quantity
2″ × 4″ × 8′ studs (for braces)	4
2″ × 6″ × 12′ boards (for sides, shelves)	6
1″ × 2″ × 8′ (for cleats)	1
8d nails	(as needed)
finish nails	(as needed)

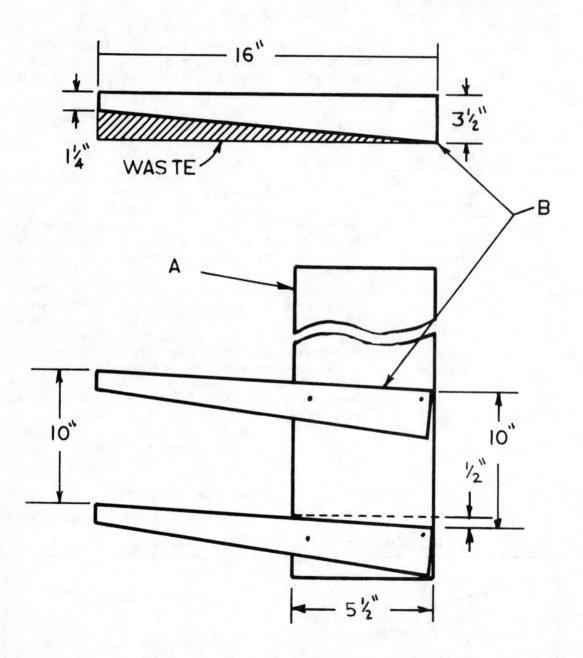

Fig. 2-19. Braces.

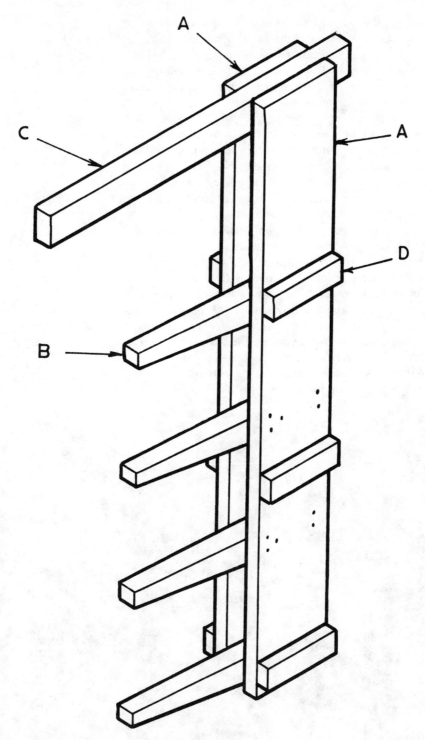

Fig. 2-20. Brace assembly.

or if the garage rafters run perpendicular to the way the stored lumber will lay, use the spacing of the joists or rafters. Push each support unit up so that its side pieces straddle the member. Nail the supports in place with five 8d nails. Do the end support units first, and then use a string or straight board to line up the middle one(s).

If the rafters run the other way, as they do for the project illustrated, cut a 2×4 an inch or two longer than the width of two rafters, plus the space between them, and put this length (part C) between a support's sides with 2 inches protruding past the back edge. Square it with a carpenter's square and secure it with five nails. Then place the unit in position on the rafters; you can select your own distance between the supports. Use spacers to square up where necessary. Nail a small cleat to the rafters on each side to eliminate lateral movement. To maintain complete rigidity, nail a 1×4 across the front (as shown in the photos).

The shelf cleats (part D) are next. Place your bottom cleats first; measure the same distance up from the floor at each of the support units. Drive one nail, and then use a square against the wall to level the cleat before driving in two more nails (Fig. 2-21). Cut a waste stick to the distance you have selected to separate the cleats on a given support unit; use it to determine the position of the next row. After those cleats are leveled (as described previously), determine the third-row location in the same manner. When all of the cleats are in place, measure for, cut, and install the shelves.

Fig. 2-21. Simple cleats hold shelving between support units. The horizontal 1×4 spanning all support units provides stability to the total system.

Now comes the enjoyable part of the project; retrieving supplies and wood stock you've had to tuck away hither and yon. Sort according to length, width, type—any way that will make your next projects easier and more enjoyable. Have fun!

PROJECT 8: SATELLITE ELECTRIC TOOL CADDY

Power tools are marvelous inventions. By simply plugging one into the proper receptacle, you can bring power to your work that would otherwise have to be accomplished by brute strength. Tedious hand sawing, drilling, sanding, and routing have all been replaced by electric hand tools. These tools make your time spent in the workshop much more enjoyable and productive.

Yet, these marvelous tools can become a source of irritation. Their power-conducting cords, at times, seem to take on a life of their own; they also tangle themselves together while we sleep. Most of us don't have really good places to keep our various power tools, and we must often search the premises just to find them. Wouldn't it be nice if you could just pull a little black box up to our work, reach in, grab the right tool, and start without a moment's waste?

That type of thinking led to the development of the satellite electric tool caddy featured in this project. Notice in Fig. 2-22 that it is, indeed, a box. It rests on four casters so that it can be easily

Fig. 2-22. A home craftsman uses the satellite electric tool caddy to provide tools and the power to use them at the worksite.

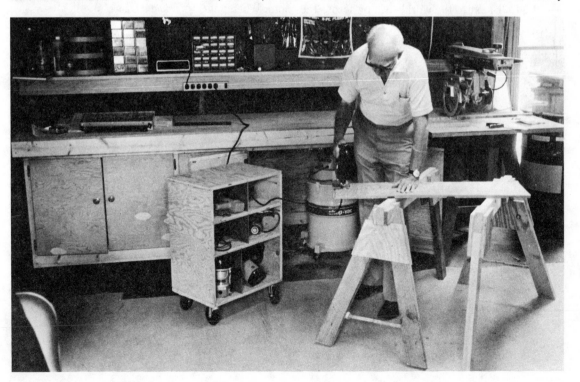

pulled about. This box has six compartments and each is a home for a specific power tool. The caddy shown, as an example, has a drill, saber saw, solder gun, power sander, router, and circular saw. Other tools can be substituted at will.

But what about that part of the dream where you simply pull the tool out and start using it? That's the secret of this box. Hidden inside it is a six-outlet power box of the type used in many shops. The power cord of each of the above tools is plugged into this power strip. By plugging the strip into the nearest power outlet, you are simultaneously plugging in all six tools. You can then select one tool at will for use. When you are through with it, simply put it back into its private little home. The individual cords are separated by quarter-inch pegboard partitions that make tangling cords an impossibility.

Another feature of this useful box can be seen in Fig. 2-23. Note that there is a 2-inch deep cavity backed by a piece of quarter-inch pegboard (which also serves as the back of the individual tool bins). Tool accessories such as blades for the saber saws and circular saws, solder, drill bits, and so on are kept here. The bins themselves are deep enough to hold other accessories—such as a complete set of router bits and an alignment accessory for the drill—behind the tools.

Portability of this box is a distinct asset in the shop. You can use it either next to the workbench or across the room. When you

Fig. 2-23. The pegboard back of the caddy holds tool accessories, plus the unit's power cord. The 2-inch inset protects them during storage in tight places.

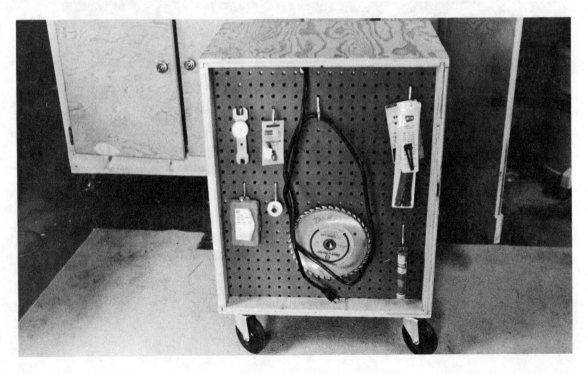

Fig. 2-24. The satellite tool caddy fits neatly in the workbench described in Project 1, keeping tools out of the way and protected until they are needed.

are through with it, just tuck it away until next time. This particular unit was sized so that it would fit perfectly into the bottomless opening of the workbench featured in Project 1. See Fig. 2-24. It sits right next to the shop vacuum.

When the doors are closed, it is completely protected from sawdust thrown by the radial-arm saw located nearby.

Doors could have been put on the front and back of the satellite tool caddy, but this would have added expense, used more space, and made it a bit harder to use. It is an option you may want to consider, however, if you have no under-the-bench storage available.

This caddy also doubles as a handy, portable work surface. A prime example is its use as a base for a drawing board (as discussed in Project 10). It can also be used to hold the lumber-sawing support described in Project 12 and undoubtedly will serve as a helping hand for many other projects.

Constructing the Caddy

The material-efficient satellite electric tool caddy uses less than a half piece of ¾-inch AC plywood, a smaller piece of quarter-inch pegboard, four casters, and a six-receptacle outlet box. See Table

2-6. Start by cutting the plywood as shown in Fig. 2-25. Each piece has additional specific dadoing and rabbeting cuts as shown in Fig. 2-26.

Start with part A (which will be one side of the box). Using a radial-arm saw or a router, make a ⅜-inch by ⅜-inch rabbet at each end on the "good" side. Turn the piece over to make additional cuts. First make a ¼-inch-wide, ⅛-inch-deep groove (Fig. 2-26) to later accept pegboard piece G. While your saw or router is set up for this groove 2 inches from the edge, it is a good idea to make the identical cut on parts B, C, and D. This will assure that the pegboard will fit properly when the four pieces are fit together.

Table 2-6. Project 8 Tools.

Saw
Hammer
Screwdriver
Expandable Bit
Router
Drill
Measuring Tape

Fig. 2-25. Plywood cuts.

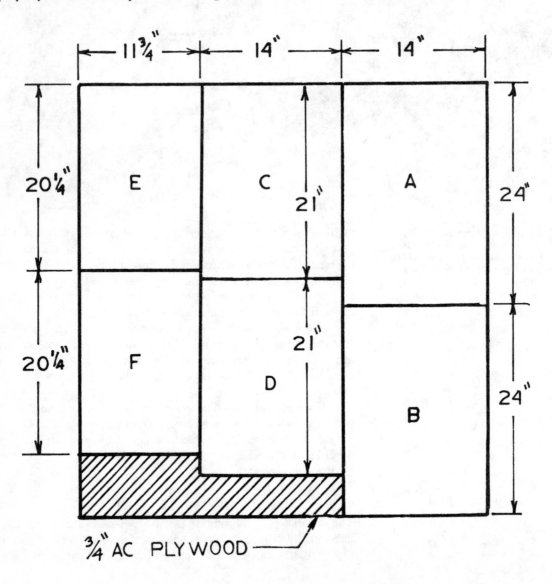

¾" AC PLYWOOD

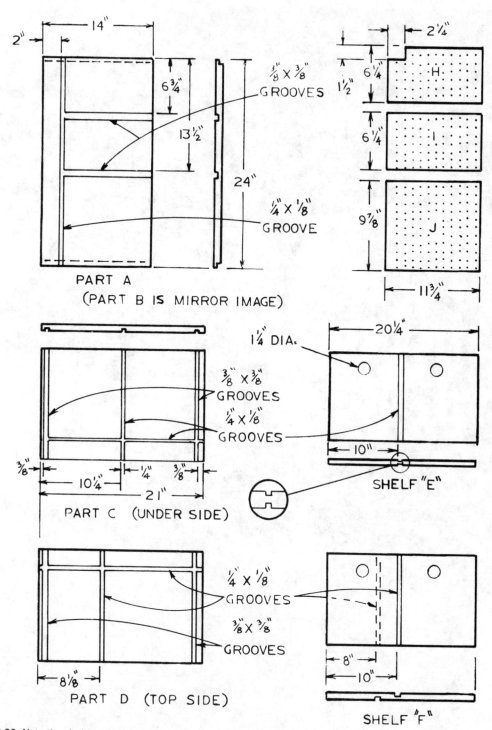

Fig. 2-26. Note the dado and rabbet cuts.

Fig. 2-27. Left: Shell dados were
cut with a radial-arm-saw-mounted
router. Note they were stopped
at the 1/4-inch groove.

Make the ¾-inch dados as shown in Fig. 2-27. The router pictured was used in a special DeWalt router attachment that provides new freedom for many operations. Notice that the dados are stopped at the quarter-inch groove so that they are not seen from the back side of the completed caddy.

Make the cuts on part B (a mirror image of part A). Do not make the very natural mistake of making identical parts or you will find yourself throwing away good plywood. When the two pieces face each other, with their good surfaces out, the various grooves and dados should be lined up perfectly.

Before going further, check the sizes of your own electric tools to make sure they will fit into the compartments shown here. Reflect differences in dimensions now on Fig. 2-26 by making changes in the positions of grooves that will hold the partitions.

If the layout shown will work for you, make these partition cuts now. The top shelf (part E) has two dados at its center, one on each surface. The top dado is to line up with the one in the top piece of part C. Shelf F (the bottom one) also has two dados, one being lined up with those in shelf E. The other is offset 2 inches to one side, on the other surface, to line up with the quarter-inch dado located in part D. Drill two holes in each shelf for the power tool cords (Fig. 2-28) and your drilling and cutting operations are completed.

It is a good idea to assemble the basic box before cutting the partitions so that fine-tune measurements can be made to assure the

Fig. 2-28. Drill holes in the back of
the two shelves to allow passage of
power cords.

93

tightest possible fit. Start by putting the side parts A and B into the bottom piece D. If you prefer, put glue into the grooves first before inserting the side pieces. Then drive finish nails up through part D into the sides. Finish by driving additional nails through the side edge of part D (through the part A and B ends that extend into the grooves). Carefully set this subassembly up on its bottom so that the side pieces extend upward.

The outlet box must be attached to the underside of part C (Fig. 2-29) so that half the outlets are on each side of the groove that will later accept a partition. The outlet box's back edge should be adjacent to the groove into which the pegboard backpiece G will fit, and the outlet box cord should exit from this side. Notch out the top of the pegboard piece G so that the cord will fit through it without binding after the caddy has been constructed.

Now is the time to put the pegboard backpiece into place. Carefully slide it down the side piece grooves. Make sure it is well seated in the part D groove. Put part C in place on top of parts A, B, and G; take care that part G seats itself properly in its groove. Before nailing part C in place, as you did part D (Fig. 2-30), make sure the shelf pieces E and F will slide into place (Fig. 2-31). If you prefer, you can put them in before attaching part C permanently.

Fig. 2-29. A power strip is attached to the underside of the unit's top, next to the groove into which the back pegboard will fit. Note that the 1/3-inch side grooves will mate with the unit's side pieces.

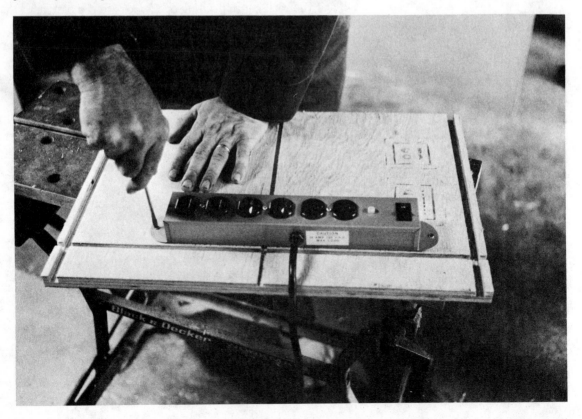

Fig. 2-30. Note corner joint that will help keep the caddy sturdy during years of use and abuse. The power cord exits through a notch cut into the pegboard back.

Make sure the fronts of the shelves are flush with the front of the box. Then drive one or two nails through the sides into the shelves to hold them into place.

It is time now to cut partitions H, I, and J. Check your construction dimensions. If they differ from those given in Fig. 2-26, reflect those differences when you measure and cut the pegboard partitions. Use Fig. 2-32 as your cutting guide for efficient use of material. Be sure to make the cutout in partition H so that the partition will slip into place around the receptacle box. See Fig. 2-33.

The basic construction is now complete. Lay the box on its back and attach the four casters. Put brass pulls on the sides to make it easier to retrieve from its hideaway place. Turn the caddy around and put in pegboard hooks to hold the various tool accessories you will need.

Starting with the bottom compartments, thread the cords up through the drilled holes in the shelves and plug them into the power box. If you need a tool someplace else, it is a simple matter to unplug it and take it away.

After you have loaded your caddy, put it into an out-of-the-way place where you can get at it readily for use. A good spot might be in

95

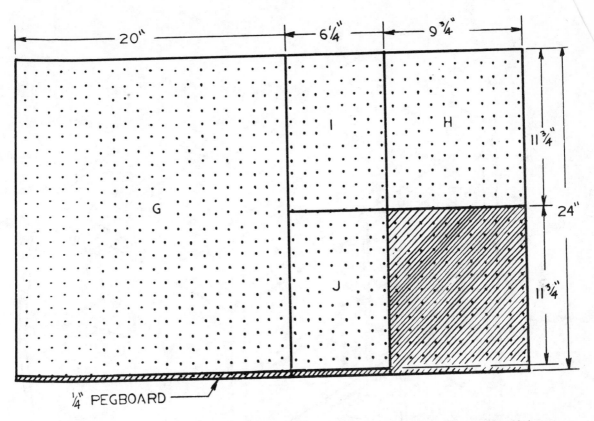

Fig. 2-32. Cutting guide.

Fig. 2-31. Left: The shelves slide into place in the side piece dados. Make sure they fit properly before nailing on the top piece.

a corner so that the wall protects the tools. You could put it between a wall and another piece of shop furniture or equipment, such as your workbench or a cabinet.

But keep it handy. You'll find yourself using it often. It will help you complete your projects with fewer problems. That certainly is a laudable achievement!

PROJECT 9: SCRAP LUMBER BIN

Does your scrap lumber pile look like an explosion just took place?

If you are the typical home craftsman, you undoubtedly have such an unruly pile. Those board ends, simply too good to throw away, represent an investment that could be recouped on this project. Trying to keep track of scrap pieces is difficult. The one piece you need is invariably on the bottom of the stack and, good intentions or not, the neat pile soon becomes a mess.

The scrap lumber bin shown in Fig. 2-34 is one answer to that keep-it-or-not dilemma. It features four separate compartments. Two of them are sized to hold 1-x-4 or 2-x-4-inch lumber; that is probably the most prevalent size of lumber in your shop. The other two compartments will hold lumber under 6½ inches wide (which

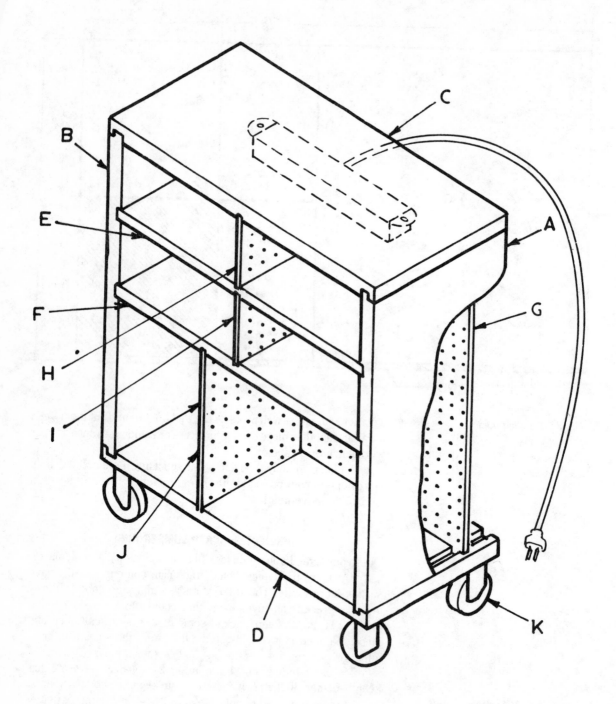

Fig. 2-33. Construction details.

Fig. 2-34. A scrap bin such as this one can help turn your throw-away end pieces into valuable ingredients in your next project. The bin was made from one 4- ×-8 piece of plywood.

will certainly include most of the rest of your scrap). Notice in the illustrations that wider pieces, such as plywood, can simply be turned sideways in one of these compartments.

A good feature of this scrap lumber bin is that it will hold any length lumber you are likely to store. Because the shop it is used in has a wall-mounted lumber rack (see Project 7), the bin is used for lumber shorter than the distance between the wall rack's braces. A combination of the wall rack, the lumber bin, and the panel rack featured on the panel saw (Project 6) compactly and efficiently holds all the lumber used in the shop. Notice that the lumber is kept in a sorted-by-size arrangement. This makes it easy to note at a glance the sizes available. It is easy to put new stock in its proper size category in order to keep the system working.

This handy bin is made up of one piece of ¾-inch AC plywood. See Table 2-7. The layout shown in Figs. 2-35, 2-36A, and 2-36B indicates how optimum use of the panel is made. Start your project by first cutting the piece into the four vertical 24-inch-wide sections. Because your saw blade does take up space, and three cuts will take some stock with them, measure carefully so that all four pieces are of identical width after being cut. The bin shown was made from three pieces cut to 23⅞ inches (reflecting an ⅛-inch-thick blade) and the fourth piece was trimmed to that size.

Cut the individual parts from the stock. That is cut C from F, A from E, B from C, and D, H, and I from each other. The three diagonal cuts were made on the panel saw shown in Fig. 2-37A. Of course, they can also be made with a circular saw on a pair of sawhorses.

Identify the best "matched pair" of pieces to serve as the outside of the bin—pieces A and E—and put these aside for the moment. They must be mirror images of each other (with the "good" surfaces on opposite sides).

Trim ⅜ of an inch of stock from the sides and bottom of the three remaining pieces—B, C, and D—as shown in Fig. 2-37B. These three pieces are to fit into three dadoes.

Note in Fig. 2-36B that piece I, when turned, fit perfectly with piece H to form a square. Put it into this position, and then trim ¾ of an inch from the combination (as shown in Fig. 2-37).

The next step is to make the dadoes in pieces F, G, H, and I. You can make them with a router, a dado blade in your radial-arm saw or, if you prefer, with several passes of a regular blade. All three pieces have identical cuts. Pieces F and G have ⅜-inch rabbets on two edges of the reverse side, and the H-I combination has a ⅜-inch rabbet on all four sides. Make the rabbets on the "bad" side of parts F and G. Because H and I will not be seen, it is immaterial which side the dadoes are on.

When you have your saw or router set up to make the dadoes,

Table 2-7. Project 9 Tools.

Saw
Hammer
Square
Router
Measuring Tape
Level

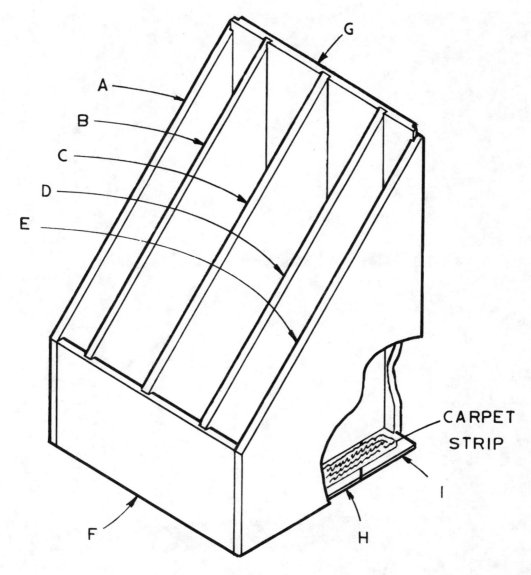

CARPET
STRIP

Fig. 2-35. Bin layout.

lay parts F, G, and H end to end on a nearby work surface, as shown in Fig. 2-37. Then take part G to your saw or router and make the first pass of one side dado, located 4⅜ of an inch from one edge. Assuming that you are using a router, make only an ⅛-inch-deep pass now; then turn the piece around and make an identical pass on the opposite side. Lay part G down on the work surface, pick up part H, and make the same passes on both sides of it (a dado should be made in part I at the same time you make the matching one in part H to make sure they will later match). Make similar passes on both sides of F. Then reset your router for an ⅛ of an inch deeper and repeat this process twice until the ⅜-inch depth has been reached.

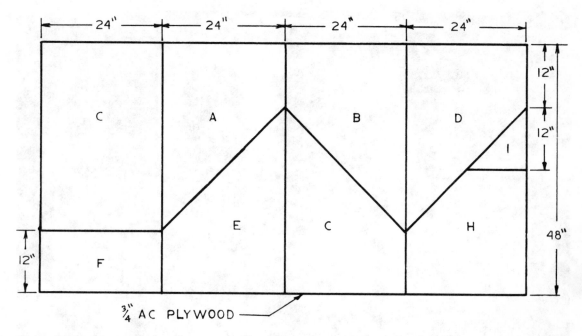

Fig. 2-36B. To ensure that pieces will fit together properly in assembly, make identical dado cuts in each board with one router setting. Notice how the small triangle piece fits in the bottom in order to make best use of your plywood sheet.

Carefully measure for the center dado and cut it ⅛ of an inch in depth at a time for all three pieces (Fig. 2-38). When you lay the pieces end to end, you will note that they match perfectly. They must do so in order to accept the partitions B, C, and D.

The last dadoing operation is to make ⅜-inch grooves in pieces A and E. They must be exactly ⅜ of an inch in from the top and both sides (Fig. 2-37). Be as careful as possible with all measurements; everything must fit well together.

It is a good idea, before nailing anything, to assemble the box in its entirety in a "dry run." Then make whatever adjustments are needed and separate the pieces. After you have done that, you will be ready to nail the pieces together.

The first step is to cut a piece of scrap carpeting into strips and nail them to piece H (as shown in Fig. 2-39). Be sure to leave space between them and at the ends of the strips for joining the wood pieces. These carpet strips will keep the stored scrap stock ends from slipping on the bin floor, protect them from unnecessary damage, and muffle the wood-on-wood sounds in the process.

Now attach part F to part H. Be sure the dadoes are lined perfectly. The center one could be slightly off if you have turned one of the pieces 180 degrees with respect to the other. After aligning both edges, drive three or four long finish nails through F into the tongue of piece H. Now turn this subassembly around and attach G to H and I in a like manner.

Put partitions B, C, and D into their respective grooves in the F-G-H assembly; make sure they are completely seated in all the

Fig. 2-36A. Left: Bin layout.

Fig. 2-37A. The angle cuts can be made on a panel saw or in a traditional manner on your sawhorses. To avoid problems later, make sure the cuts are accurate.

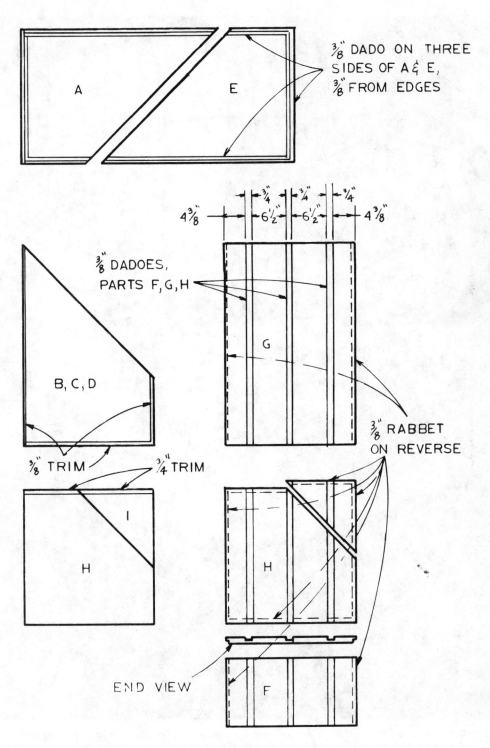

Fig. 2-37B. Bin details.

Fig. 2-38. Remove only 1/8-inch at a time with your router in order to avoid burning and chipping the wood and dulling your bit. Cut both edge pieces at the same setting. Then measure carefully for the center groove.

Fig. 2-39. Carpet strips will help hold wood stock in place, lessen damage, and help provide a quieter surrounding. Be sure to leave space around each piece for joints between wood surfaces.

dadoes. Put finish nails into the partitions through pieces F, G, and H in order to hold them in place.

Turn this new assembly over so that an edge of the F-G-H box is lying on the floor. Place part A (or E) over it so that the assembly's tongue will fit into the dado made in the three edges of the side piece. Tap these edges with a hammer to make sure they are perfectly seated; then nail the side into place as before. Turn the box over and repeat the procedure with the other side (Fig. 2-40).

That completes the construction of the lumber bin. If you prefer, you can put tack-glides under the bin. Nail them into the corners of H-I to elevate the bin slightly in the event of wet floors. The bin can also be painted.

It is time now to load the bin with your scrap lumber. It is also a good time to throw away the pieces that you have no chance of using. Sort according to size, type of lumber, or whatever criteria you prefer. You'll suddenly find your work area neat again. With only a very little effort, you can keep it that way, thanks in part to your new bin.

Fig. 2-40. Nail the side pieces on last. Accurate cutting is imperative for a proper fit.

PROJECT 10: WALL-HUNG DRAWING CABINET

Of course you should have a drawing table. Potential projects that look good in daydreams too often become nightmares during construction because of no concrete plans to follow. A drawing table and its accessories provide the tools you need to make the dream reality. See Table 2-8.

Making drawings in a workshop is not without its problems. An in-progress drawing on an exposed drawing board, and the drawing accessories lying nearby, seem to work as powerful sawdust magnets and they must constantly be cleaned. Putting everything away between drawing sessions outwardly seems to be the answer, but that is a lot of work that should be eliminated if possible.

The wall-hung drawing cabinet shown in Fig. 2-41 is very simple to construct. The only materials needed are an 8-foot piece of 1-×-6 pine (the same used for the lumber storage rack in Project 7), an identical length of 1-×-2 or 1-×-3 pine, and a small piece of ¼-inch-thick or ⅛-inch-thick pegboard. A handful of nails and two screws complete the materials list for the basic box.

The front cover for the box is your drawing board (Figs. 2-42 and 2-43). Notice in Fig. 2-44 that it is specially outfitted with two doorstops (part G) and two rubber furniture tack slides (part H). When it is to be used, the drawing board is placed on a flat surface. The two doorstops are at the far side between the drawing board and the table surface. They provide a tilt to the drawing board that makes it easy to use, and the rubber tips keep the board solidly in place. The dimensions in Fig. 2-44 show the locations of the feet if the board is to be used on a small surface, such as the top of the satellite electric tool caddy (Project 8), as in Fig. 2-41 where the front of the board will hang over the edge. If you plan to use a surface where the board will not hang over, move the rubber tack glides closer to the edge to keep the board edge above the table surface.

The dimensions given in the drawings and in the materials list assume your drawing board is 21¼ inches by 26 inches. You can certainly substitute a different-sized board; keep in mind that you must adjust for these sizes. For example, if the length is 24 inches rather than 26 inches, just deduct 2 inches from the lengths of the horizontal box pieces. See Table 2-9.

Constructing the Cabinet

The first step is to make the rabbets in the two C parts so they will accept opposite edges of the drawing board. They should be the thickness of your board and extend ⅜ of an inch below the surface of the part. Notice that the side pieces are not rabbeted. It might be easier to make the rabbets before the two C parts are separated.

After making any necessary size adjustments reflecting a variance in your drawing board size, cut the rest of the pieces to length.

Fig. 2-42. A drawing can remain on the board and be protected from sawdust. The doorstops and furniture glides hold the board at the comfortable working angle, when in use, and keeps it from sliding.

Fig. 2-41. Left: The cabinet and drawing board, used in conjunction with the satellite electric tool caddy featured in Project 8, provides an ideal drawing setup. The drawing board becomes the front for the cabinet.

Then make a four-sided unit with the two C parts and the two D parts (Fig. 2-43) with the rabbets facing each other. The C parts should be inside the D parts (Fig. 2-44). See Figs. 2-45 and 2-46.

Hold this box up on the wall on which it will later hang in order to determine the best location. When you have found it, position part A beneath the top C part. Remove the box, level the part A with a spirit level, and then attach it to the wall. If the wall is of stud-and-wallboard construction, be sure the nails at each end are driven into the studs. If the width of your box is narrower than the distances between the studs, use toggle bolts for its attachment. You should position the box so that one part B will later lie over a stud.

With the top part A in place, set the box on it so that it rests on the top edge. Use a carpenter's square to make sure the box is square (Fig. 2-47). Now put the other part A in the bottom of the box so one edge lays on the box's part C; nail part A into place on the wall. It is now easy to locate and attach the two parts B between the ends of the two parts A. Make sure they are snug against the box's side parts (B).

Use small finish nails to attach the box to this nailed-on frame. Drive two or three nails from each side and the top and bottom (through the C and D parts into the A and B parts). When that has

Fig. 2-43. The cabinet is a simple four-sided frame made from 1- ×-6 material. Note the use of a stop built into the bench, featured in Project 1.

Fig. 2-44. The top and bottom boards are rabbeted to accept the drawing board. The dark line on the right piece is a mark in the wood itself; it is not a cut made for this project.

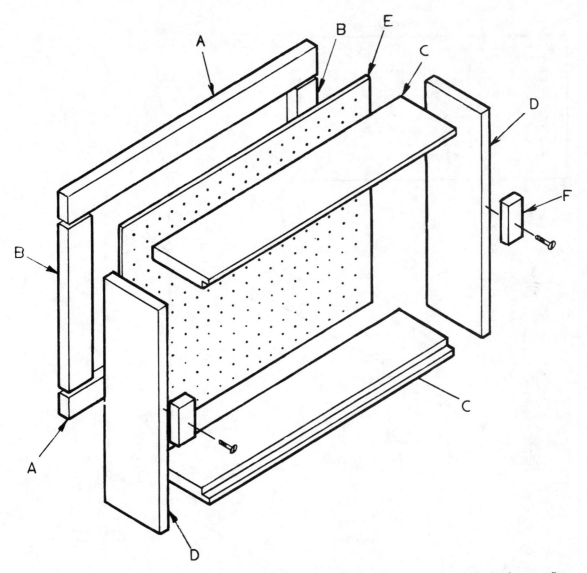

Fig. 2-45. Drawing board details.

been completed, insert pegboard E, attach it with the four roofing nails, and the basic structure is complete.

The only remaining parts are the two 4-inch-long pieces that hold the drawing board in place in the cabinet front. Notice that a hole is driven off center in each so that, when turned to one position, the board can be easily removed and replaced. When turned 180 degrees from this position, however, these pieces form a lip that hold the board in place.

Storing Drawing Accessories

Install pegboard hooks on which to hang your triangles, templates,

Table 2-9. Project 10 Bill of Materials.

Part	Dimensions	Quantity
A	¾" × 2½" × 26¼" pine	2
B	¾" × 2½" × 16" pine	2
C	¾" × 5½" × 26¼" pine	2
D	¾" × 5½" × 22¼" pine	2
E	20" × 26½" pegboard	1
F	¾" × 1½" × 4" pine	2
G	3" long door stop	2
H	Rubber tack glide	2

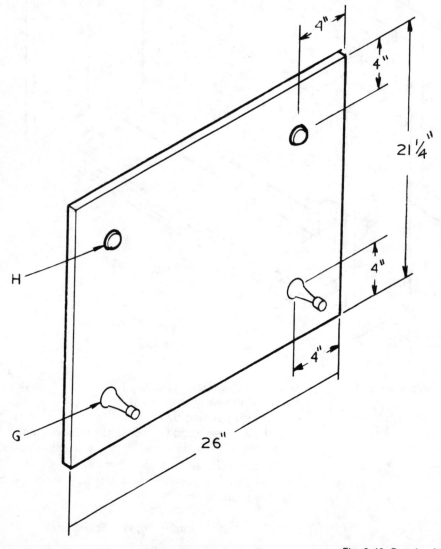

Fig. 2-46. Drawing board details.

Fig. 2-47. Nail narrow frame pieces to the wall first, and then slip the cabinet frame over it. Use a carpenter's square to ensure a square cabinet.

and similar accessories. The inside bottom surface of the box (part C) can serve as a shelf for frequently used accessories such as pencils and pens, pointers, ink, dividers, and so on. If you prefer, you can lay a pad of paper on the edge in this cavity before putting the drawing board in place.

Two nails driven into the wall beneath the cabinet will provide a handy support for your T-square. Another nail will give you easy access to your drawing brush. This brush can be used in the shop to keep surfaces free of sawdust.

Notice that a drawing taped to the drawing board can remain there and the drawing board can be put away and later retrieved as many times as is necessary to complete the drawing. If there is no drawing on the board, you can reverse the board and put it "feet first" into its storage home, eliminating the projections from the unit.

This cabinet will keep your materials and drawings free of sawdust. You will never again have to get out and put away the various drawing instruments and accessories each time you want to draw (and put them away when you are interrupted). In the process, you will be better able to plan your projects on paper and reduce construction mistakes and frazzled tempers. More enjoyment and fewer problems . . . what more could a home craftsman want?

3

Work Center
Tools and Fixtures

DURING THE PAST SEVERAL EPOCHS, MAN HAS MADE TWO very major steps forward. One was to invent the wheel; this allowed automobiles to be invented and therefore made trips to the hardware store easier. The other major step was to devise a portable work center.

The home handyman has taken to the work center like a duck to water. At least three major manufacturers are making them. And small wonder. The center provides a sturdy base upon which to work, holds a multitude of things in a multitude of ways, and is portable. It can be taken to the job, used, then perhaps hung upon a wall until the next time it is needed.

It is so ingenious that it can be used in many ways that are not at first readily evident. You will just scratch the surface, so to speak, by using it only to hold something steady. Most of the projects in this chapter will provide you with new ways to multiply its use in almost any home workshop situation.

Take a moment now to thumb through this chapter and look at each project with a calculating eye. Will the projects make your workshop experience more enjoyable or easier? If the balance swings to the "yes" side, you can squeeze even more utility out of your work center. If you don't have one yet, perhaps it should be your very next workshop acquisition.

PROJECT 11: PORTABLE TOOL AND FIXTURE RACK

The list of potential work center tools is so long that this first project is presented as a way to "hold it all." It is a portable accessories rack with several major features. Perhaps most obvious are the seven sets of arms, or braces that extend from it to hold odd-shaped, versatile accessories with ease (Fig. 3-1). Without such a system, these accessories would have to be tucked away under tables, hung on walls, hidden in closets, or stuck into drawers. In general, they would present a very untidy appearance. The rack keeps them all in one spot where they can be reached handily. That's only one of several features of this rack.

Turn the rack around on its big wheels and you'll notice a large storage area with two handy shelves in the lower half and an open area at the top (Figs. 3-2 and 3-3). The whole thing is backed with a quarter-inch pegboard designed to hold other shop accessories. Notice that it has no doors. When the rack is not being used, it is pushed against a wall so that the wall itself serves to close the opening. When it is in this position, it very much resembles the lumber storage rack (Project 7).

Preparing the Materials

This rack uses materials very efficiently. A 4-×-8-foot sheet of ¾-inch AC plywood, some 2×4s, a half sheet of pegboard, and a set of four swivel wheels are the basic ingredients. See Table 3-1.

First cut the plywood following the layout shown in Figs. 3-4A, 3-4B, and 3-5. Cut the panel in half longways; then cut each of these pieces in half, again longways. Although the widths of these four pieces are marked 12 inches in Fig. 3-4, each piece will be a fraction of an inch narrower because of the thickness of the three saw kerfs. Cut carefully so that each piece will be of equal width.

Cut the "C" pieces from the "A" pieces (making them a full 27¼ inches long). These will be the top and bottom pieces of the rack. The remaining parts (parts "A") will form the inside side walls of the rack. Now cut parts D from parts B. Cut the remaining "scrap" piece in two, lengthwise, to form four part E cleats that will later hold the shelves.

Cut the 14 braces (G) using the tapering jig described in Project 19. Cut the 12-inch-long parts H and parts F from 2×4s. Cut part F as shown in Fig. 3-6.

Assembling the Rack

Lay one part A down flat on the floor (remember that A is the shorter of the side pieces) and put parts F and H into place. Hold them with nails that extend through them and into part A, yet do not protrude

Table 3-1. Project 11 Tools.

Saw
Hammer
Screwdriver
Square
Drill
Measuring Tape

Fig. 3-1. This rack was designed to hold work-center accessories, but also features ample storage behind it for other tools and materials. To "close" the cabinet, simply roll it next to a wall.

Fig. 3-2. The front of the rack.

Fig. 3-3. The back of the rack.

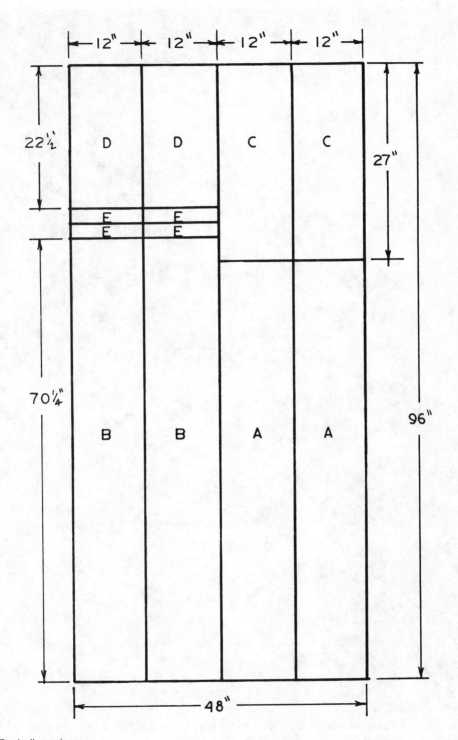

Fig. 3-4A. Rack dimensions.

Fig. 3-4B. Tack braces to a short side piece after angling them as shown in Fig. 3-6. The notch in piece F, in the foreground, will later accept a cross piece that will hold two casters.

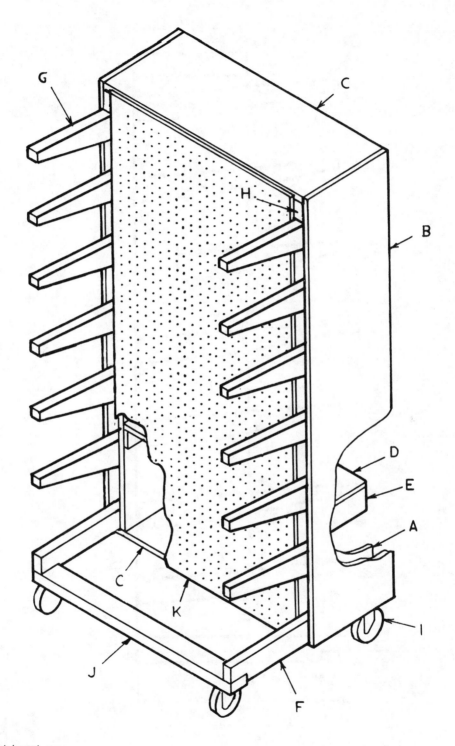

Fig. 3-5. Rack layout.

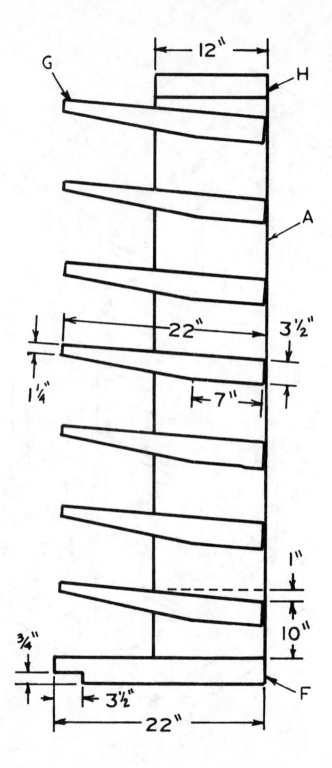

Fig. 3-6. Brace positions.

through that side piece. You will nail the seven side braces in the same fashion (Fig. 3-4). This assembly method will make certain the pieces hold their position until proper nails are driven through them from the outside of parts A and B.

Follow Fig. 3-6 to place the braces. Starting with the upper edge of part F, measure, and mark every 10 inches on one edge of part A. Use a carpenter's square to make identical marks on the opposite side (that is, on the left side of the same surface) and then measure up 1 inch from each of these latter marks. This is the meaningful mark; erase or cross through the marks under them made only to find the latter's positions.

Again following Fig. 3-6, lay a part G across part A so that its narrow end lies to the left, beyond the left edge of part A. The top right corner should be at the first 10-inch mark on the right-hand side, and the upper surface of G should be right on the "meaningful" mark just described. Drive two short nails through the piece into part A (as previously described). Attach the other six braces in a similar manner.

With this done, you are now ready to put part B (the longer "side part") into place. Lay it on top of the braces, with its long edges parallel to those of part A, so that it extends ¾ of an inch at the top and bottom (Fig. 3-7). Check all measurements carefully and then nail part B in place. Drive at least two nails through part B into the seven braces, part F and part H. Turn the assembly over now and drive two or more nails through each 2×4 position on that side. You now have a sandwich made of plywood (a 2×4 and then plywood).

Make the other rack side in a similar fashion; remember that it is a mirror image of the first side. Lay part A down and then put parts G, F and H down so that F and the G parts extend to the *right* of part A (rather than to the left as before). Follow identical assembly steps until it is completed.

The next step is to make a box from these sides, plus the two parts C. Lay the side assemblies on their back edge, the braces pointing up, and their B sides—that is, the shorter sides—facing each other. Space them so that part C will fit between the top ends of parts B and rest on the two part H 2×4s. Drive four or five nails through C into H on each side (Fig. 3-8). The top surface of C should be flush with the ends of part B. Now put the other part C at the other end of the box so that it rests on parts F. Nail it into place as before.

Next comes part J; it fits into the notches made into the two parts F. Nail this into place now. Then attach the casters to this part and to the corners of part C on the other edge (Fig. 3-9).

While the "box" is still flat in this position, cut the pegboard to size and lay it between the braces. Attach it will roofing nails,

Fig. 3-7. Make two side units so that they are mirror images to each other. Center a part B on each one so that top and bottom pieces C will fit between them when the box is constructed.

Fig. 3-8. Make the box as shown. Put extra nails through the top and the bottom, into parts H and F, to increase rigidity.

126

spaced 5 to 6 inches apart, nailed into the edges of the two C parts and the two A parts (Fig. 3-10). Be sure to drive the nails through the material itself and not through the pegboard holes. The pegboard is part of the structural makeup of the rack.

Lift the rack up onto its wheels and turn it so that the inside of the box can be seen. You might want to wait until you have a firmer idea of what you will put into this "box" before you position the shelves. The shelves in the model shown are placed 15 inches apart. Nail cleats at the appropriate height on both sides, into part A, and simply lay the shelves on them. It is not necessary to nail the shelves into position.

PROJECT 12: LUMBER SAWING SUPPORT

If ever a home craftsman feels inadequate, it is when he or she tries to cut a 16-foot board without the benefit of a 10-foot table. Jerry-rigging, stop-gap solutions, such as using a chair back or another object to hold the extended lumber, can lead to bad cuts and frayed tempers. Trying to do without a support of any kind is downright dangerous.

A standard solution offered by shop-oriented magazines and books is to build a rather complicated floor stand with an adjust-

able-height roller. It solves the problem, but it presents one of its own: storage of the stand when it is not needed.

Two simple roller stands are described in this section. One is used in conjunction with a commercially available work center (Fig. 3-11) and the other is designed for workbench top use (Fig. 3-12). The materials needed are scrap pieces of 2×4, screws or nails, and perhaps a little glue. Also see Table 3-2. The resulting devices are versatile, practical, and economical.

The central element of this roller unit is the common type of rolling pin found in almost every kitchen. It can be immediately switched from one base to another by merely picking it up and laying it down again. The bases themselves are adjustable in height and, by simply using spacers, the same one can be used in both situations.

Fig. 3-10. Attach pegboard in order to provide stability and hanger space for the inside of the cabinet. Roofing nails work well in this application.

Table 3-2. Project 12 Tools.

Saw
Hammer
Measuring Tape

Fig. 3-11. The simple sawing support simplifies sawing chores by providing a portable support that uses the work center as its base. It is equally helpful when working with dimension lumber and paneling.

The rolling pin used in the units is 3 inches in diameter and has a roller length of 15 inches. The length is not crucial for this project, but the diameter has bearing on the actual unit height. The height must be level with the saw's table surface when it is in working position.

The combination used here achieved that perfect height with only the addition of small spacers beneath the handles. Be sure to adjust base dimensions to fit the actual rolling pin you will use. Make a "dry run" with the component parts before gluing and screwing them into position (Fig. 3-12).

To make the basic unit, first cut part A (Fig. 3-13); it is 29 inches long—the width of the work center used—so it will fit the tool and fixture storage unit described in Project 11.

Cut two parts B and lay them across the first piece and equidistant from its ends so that the roller can fit between them with perhaps a quarter inch to spare at each end. The handles will each extend over one of the pieces. Cut four additional pieces of 2×4 (parts C). Place one on each side of the two handles so that it is flush with an end of the part B (upon which it rests). The resulting space between each pair forms a cradle for a rolling pin handle.

Now is the time for your dry run. Put the work center next to the saw table and place the assembly on it, *except* for part A. Its top

Fig. 3-12. The benchtop version of the sawing support uses the same rolling pin used with the work center version. Its thin profile allows it to be tucked away easily between jobs.

will eventually be flush with the work center's top; therefore it will have no bearing whatever on the roller's height. Extend a straight board over the saw table edge so that it is directly above the roller. If it touches the roller—as it does in the unit pictured—and does not lift the board from the saw table, the project is ready for assembly.

Any shortfall of up to perhaps 2 inches can be eliminated by putting wooden spacer strips under the 6-inch pieces (next to the 29-inch piece), in the cradles, or both (see Fig. 3-14). To cover somewhat wider spaces, assemble the unit with part A on edge and use a wider spacer.

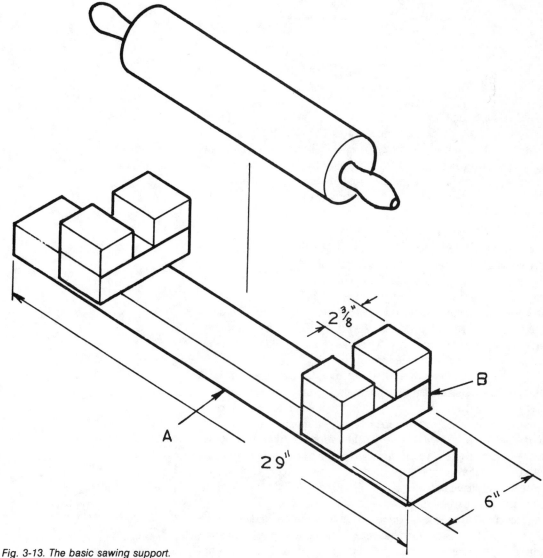

Fig. 3-13. The basic sawing support.

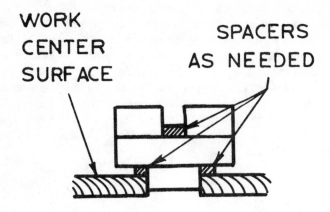

WORK
CENTER
SURFACE

SPACERS
AS NEEDED

Fig. 3-14. Installing spacers.

END VIEW

This same unit might work, unaltered or with only spacer changes made, on your workbench or another table. If it is too tall, construct a second base as shown in Figs. 3-15 and 3-16. This one can be kept permanently on or near the workbench, with the rolling pin installed, for instant use when long lumber presents a problem. The work center base can be kept on a storage rack (Project 11) until needed.

PROJECT 13: SHOOTING BOARD

Perhaps a good example of combining the old and the new is adapting a "shooting board" for use in your work center. A shooting board is a traditional type of jig, used by generations of woodworkers, for holding stock in a correct position for planing. It is used both for planing the edges of thin wood, upon which a plane might normally wobble and create a wavy surface, and for planing an edge straight and square on thicker wood.

Figure 3-17 shows the shooting (or planing) board in use. Although it appears that the plane might be touching part C (identified in Fig. 3-18A) as it planes the workpiece, that workpiece is actually overhanging the upper platform by about a quarter of an inch. The plane is held square to the workpiece because of the plane's side and sole in relation to part B, the base. Part D serves as a stop to hold the workpiece in position. Note in Fig. 3-17 a piece of waste stock is used between this stop and the workpiece in order to keep the corner from splintering.

Because of the size of the shooting board, the marriage of the old and the new was made in heaven. To be of most use, it must be large enough to handle a variety of sizes of wood. And that presents

Fig. 3-15. For sawing accuracy, make sure the saw stock is flush with both saw table and the roller. A one-time adjustment with spacers beneath the rolling pin handles is generally sufficient.

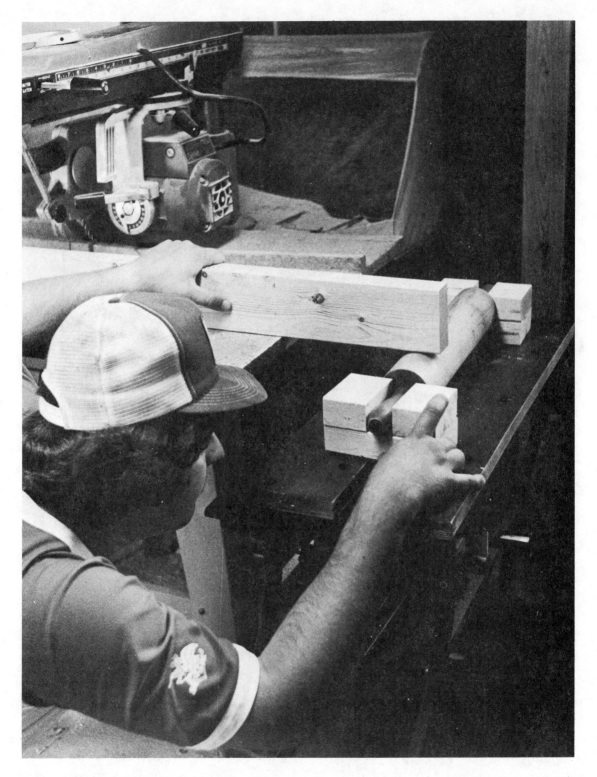

133

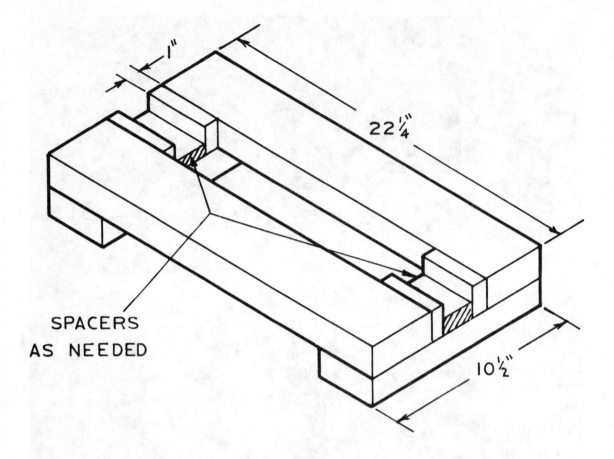

SPACERS
AS NEEDED

storage problems. After the workpiece has been planed, the craftsman need only hang this jig, by its 2-×-4 base, onto the fixture rack described in Project 11. It must also be held steady while the craftsman holds this wood on it with one hand and moves the plane with the other. This is a function that the work center very handily accomplishes.

You will find this an easy project to complete. See Table 3-3. First cut parts B, C, and D from ¾-inch AC plywood. Lightly sand the edges to remove any splinters. Drill and countersink 3/16-inch holes through parts B, C, and D (as shown in Fig. 3-18B).

Cut a 2×4 to a 29-inch length to form part A and lay it on your work surface. Place part B on it so that it is centered lengthwise and the back edges of A and B are flush (with the three drilled holes positioned over part A). If you prefer put white glue between the pieces. With a 9/32-inch-diameter drill bit, drill starter holes down through the holes in part B, into part A, and turn in the 10-×-1¼ screws until their tops are at or below the part B surface.

Fig. 3-16. A second base for support.

Table 3-3. Project 13 Tools.

Saw
Screwdriver
Countersink Bit
Router
Drill
Clamps
Measuring Tape

134

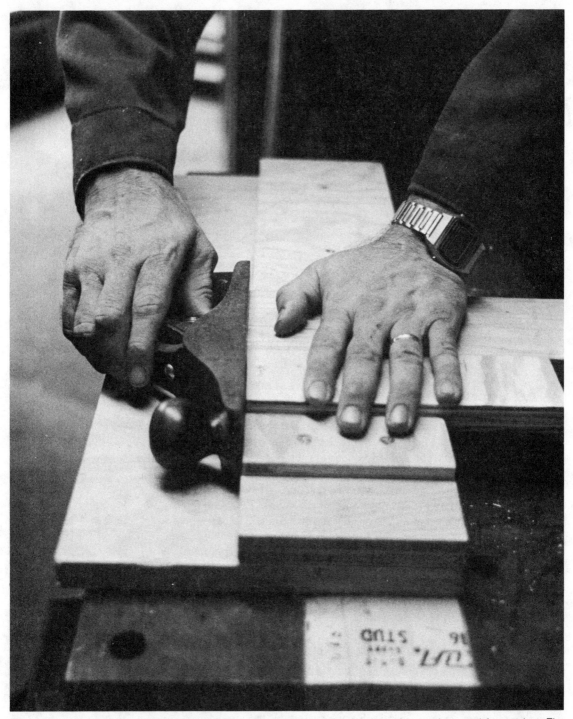

Fig. 3-17. An attached 2 × 4 holds this shooting board solidly in place, helping the craftsman plane stock for a project. The unit hangs conveniently from the tool and fixture rack described in Project 11.

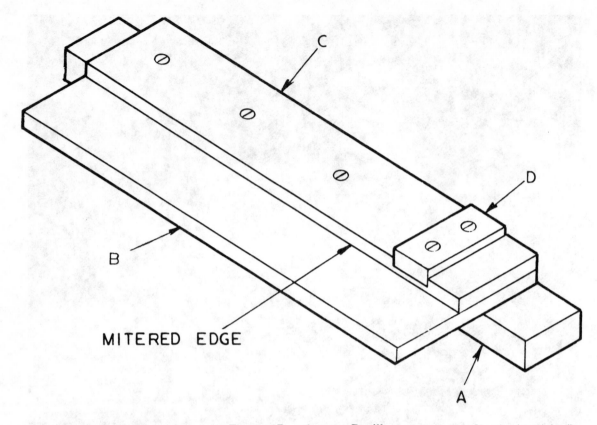

C

D

B

MITERED EDGE

A

Cut a dado in part C, as shown in Fig. 3-18B so that part D will fit snugly into it. You can use either a router or a radial-arm saw to make this cut. Bevel the bottom edge opposite the edge that will later be flush with the edge of part B (as shown in Fig. 3-19). The bevel will later provide a place for sawdust and small shavings to escape. It will therefore promote accuracy of the cut as the plane glides along part B against part C. Now glue and clamp part C to part B, as shown in the illustrations, and insert its screws.

Position part D into the dado made in part C (Fig. 3-20) so that the edges are even. Clamp this into place and drill starter holes as before. Then drive the two screws home. This completes the assembly of the shooting board and it takes you one step closer to pleasurable and accurate woodworking.

PROJECT 14: PORTABLE MECHANIC'S VISE

Whatever your specialty, you can hardly do without a mechanic's vise. Many craftsmen think of a vise as second only in importance to the workbench. After they have built their bench, attaching a vise is often the next step taken. A vise is the one basic tool that almost demands that work come to it.

Fig. 3-18A. Shooting board details.

Fig. 3-18B. Shooting board parts.

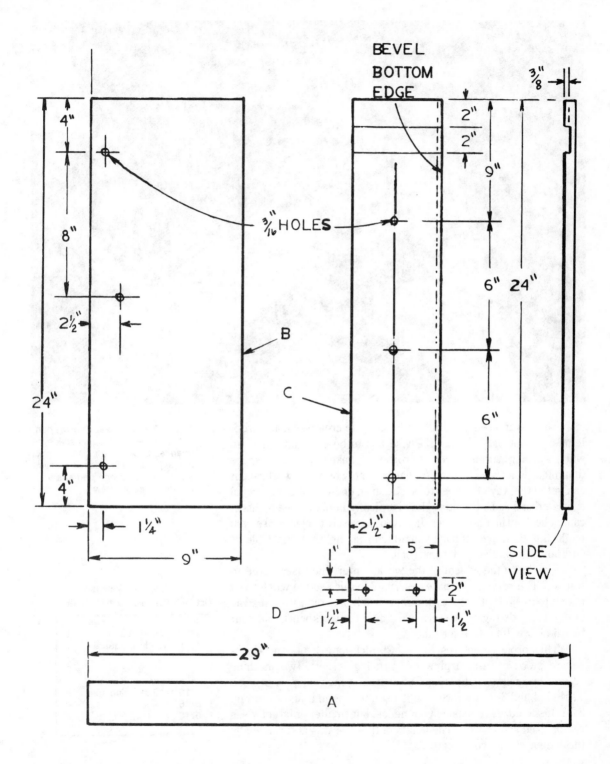

BEVEL
BOTTOM
EDGE

3/8"

4"

8"

2 1/2"

B

24"

4"

1 1/4"

9"

3/16" HOLES

2"

2"

9"

6"

24"

6"

C

2 1/2"

5

SIDE
VIEW

1"

2"

D

1 1/2"

1 1/2"

29"

A

137

This natural reflex action might serve to create as many problems as it solves. For one, the vise has to be constantly dodged when working with all kinds of projects. It takes up surface space that might otherwise be used for flat assembly or detail work, and it can get in the way of lumber to be cut on an end-of-the-bench radial saw. Perhaps as bad, bolting the vise firmly in place means that it cannot be used in other places. If you opt for a screw-clamp vise, you might find that, even though you attach it as tightly as possible, it will not hold in place for some jobs.

Thanks to the advent of the work center, the vise is free to wander. The very simple base described in this section will let you take it to the job with the work center, use it, and then store it away until it is needed again. You can use it near the workbench, but your bench also will be free for other use.

This project requires only a 29-inch-long 2×4, an 8-inch-square piece of ¾-inch plywood, two lag screws, two machine screws and nuts, washers and, of course, a mechanic's vise. See Table 3-4 and 3-5. A 4-inch vise is used for the unit shown in Fig. 3-21. It should serve most of your needs, but smaller or larger vises can be used just as well. The length of the 2×4 was determined by the length of the work center.

Fig. 3-19. Bevel the edge of the part C to provide a sawdust escape channel. In use, the plane will not actually touch this piece, it will slide along the workpiece perhaps a quarter of an inch away.

Table 3-4. Materials List for a Portable Mechanic's Vise.

1¾″ × 3¾″ × 29″	1
¾″ plywood, 8″ square	1
4″ vise	1
⅜″ × 2½″ lag screw	2
⅜″ washer	2
5/16 × 18 machine screw	2
5/16″ washer	4
5/16″ × 18 nut	2

Fig. 3-20. Apply glue between the pieces, and then clamp them solidly together until dry. The hand holds the stop that will hold the workpiece firmly in place while its edge is being planed.

Cut the plywood to size. Then draw lines midway across the piece, in both directions, to form four quadrants (Fig. 3-22). Place the vise on the approximate center of the piece, bottom side next to its surface, and move it about until the lines are centered in the four holes. Carefully insert your pencil into each hole, draw a circle (using the vise hole as your guide), and remove the vise.

To assure the strongest possible attachment of the vise to the base, two of the holes are lined up so that ⅜-inch-diameter lag screws can slip through the plywood and screw into the 2×4. Drill ⅜-inch holes in these two positions and 5/16-inch holes in the other two positions (Fig. 3-23) to later accept 5/16-18×1½-inch machine screws (see Fig. 3-24). Turn the plywood piece over and either cut a trough for the machine screw nuts and washers in order to keep them above the work center surface or route concentric, larger-diameter holes for the same purpose.

Turn the piece right side up once again and center it both lengthwise and widthwise on the 2×4. Clamp or hold it firmly in position, pass the ¼-inch drill bit down through the ⅜-inch holes, and drill centered holes that will accept the lag screws. Place the vise in position. Put a washered lag screw through the vise support hole and the plywood holes. With a wrench, turn the screws into the 2×4 until snug.

Cut the machine screws to their proper lengths so that their ends will not touch the work center surface after assembly (the lengths depend in part upon the vise support thickness). With this

Table 3-5. Project 14 Tools.

| Saw |
| Router |
| Drill |
| Measuring Tape |
| Pliers |

Fig. 3-21. The work-center vise in use. Note that the craftsman has access to the vise from both sides. This is certainly an advantage over a workbench-mounted vise. When its job is completed, the vise will be stored away for future use.

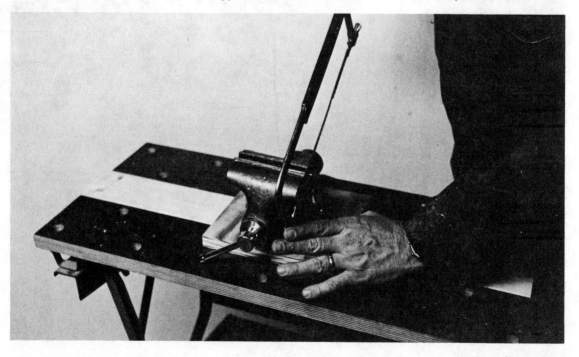

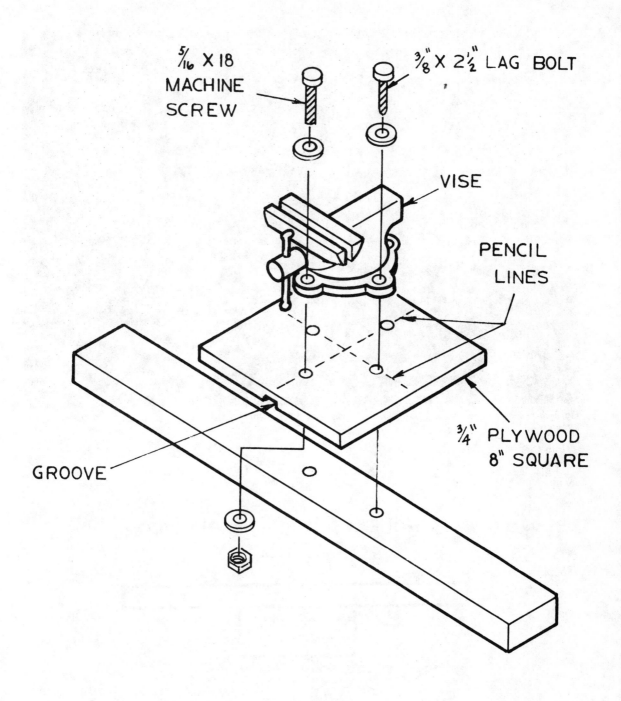

$\frac{5}{16}$ X 18 MACHINE SCREW

$\frac{3}{8}$" X $2\frac{1}{2}$" LAG BOLT

VISE

PENCIL LINES

$\frac{3}{4}$" PLYWOOD 8" SQUARE

GROOVE

Fig. 3-22. Details of a portable mechanic's vise.

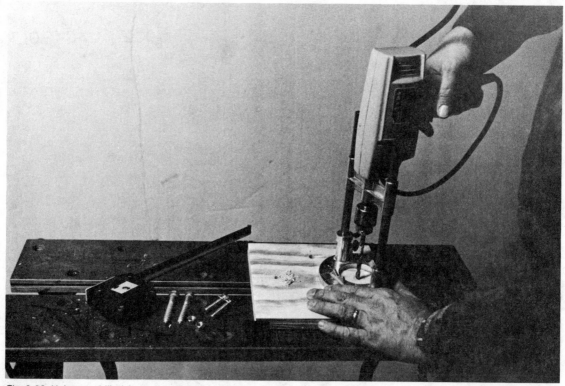

Fig. 3-23. Holes are drilled through the 8-inch square plywood piece so that both lag bolts and machine bolts can be slipped through.

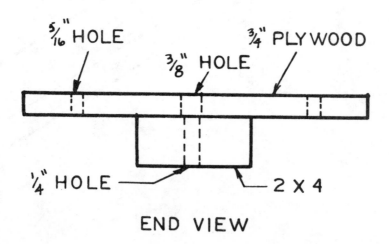

Fig. 3-24. Attaching the vise base.

Fig. 3-25. Notice the dado in the plywood piece made to allow clearance for the two machine screw nuts. Two lag bolts were used to hold the vise and plywood to the 2 × 4, thereby increasing the holding power and thus the utility of the vise.

143

done, insert the washered machine bolts through the vise support and the plywood. Put the washers onto the bolts and tighten on the nuts (Fig. 3-25).

Now store the vise away on your work center accessory rack until you have need for it. You've just solved problems you might have faced again and again for the rest of your life. You can now take the vise to the work and keep your workbench clear for more important things.

PROJECT 15: DOUBLE LAZY SUSAN

There comes a time when every home craftsmen absolutely needs a revolving work surface. For some, that time comes when in-process sculptures must be constantly revolved and revised to achieve proper likenesses (Fig. 3-26). For electronics buffs and other kit hobbyists, the need might occur during an assembly operation.

The double lazy Susan answers those basic needs and does much more besides. Notice it has *two* revolving surfaces. Therefore you can have two projects going on at one time. The device is specifically designed for use with a work center. Because the two lazy Susans extend beyond a work center end, it allows craftsmen to

Fig. 3-26. The double lazy Susan fits snugly into the portable work center, providing handy turntables for objects as heavy as these plaster sculptures. The device is invaluable in many workshop situations.

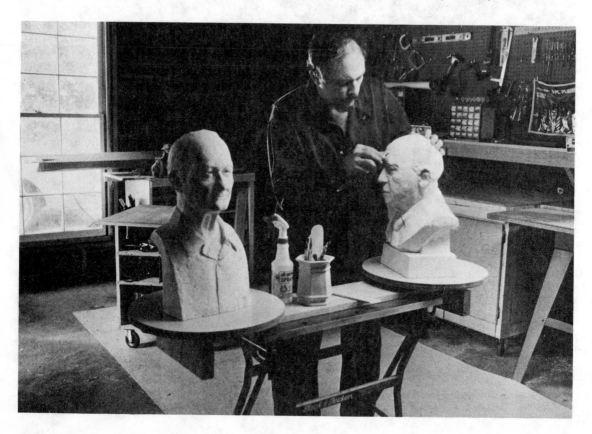

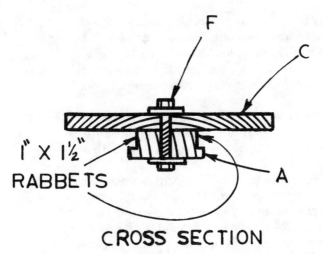

F

C

1" X 1½"
RABBETS

A

CROSS SECTION

Fig. 3-27. A cross section of the
rabbet cut.

sit in comfort at each end while working. Two craftsmen can work there simultaneously.

Notice that there is a "foot" at each end, under the surfaces, that allows you to put the device on a table or workbench. You can work with it there and, if you prefer, you can use the double turntable to display your products. Those who exhibit in shows will find it very easy to cover the framework with cloth. This leaves only the rotating surfaces to be seen by the public.

Only common materials are used for this work aid. The two rotating surfaces are laminated countertop cutouts purchased at $1 each from a local cabinetmaker. You undoubtedly will have a source for these in your own area, but if not they can be cut from standard ¾-inch plywood and they can be painted or covered with contact paper or another protective or decorative surface. The other materials include a 3-foot, 6-inch length of 1-×-8 shelving, a 3-foot, 3-inch long 2×4, two 1-foot long 2×4s, three 5/16-×-3-inch bolts with nuts and six washers. The two boat seat swivels can be obtained from either a marine supply house or your local hardware store. If the dealer does not have them in stock, he can undoubtedly order them from his supplier. See Table 3-6.

Start by cutting parts A and B to length from a 2×4. Cut a 1-inch-deep by ½-inch-wide rabbet on each side of part A (see Fig. 3-27) with your saw or router. The work center's moveable ¾-inch-thick top will later fit into these rabbets, and the lips will provide holding power to assure that the turntable set will not twist out of the work center when a heavy weight is put on one end.

Cut part C to length, center part A on one side, and clamp the two together. Drill three 5/16-inch holes through those pieces. Drill one through the center and the others about 9 inches from each end of part B, where they will be hidden by the 18-inch-diameter turntable.

Table 3-6. Project 15 Tools.

Saw
Hammer
Screwdriver
Router
Drill
Clamps
Adjustable Wrench
Measuring Tape

Set this assembly on the two "feet" (part B), one at each end. Center part C on them and drive two nails down through parts B at each end. Make sure the nails are not located where the turntable's screws will later be positioned. Drive another nail through part B into the end of part A in order to complete the base assembly. See Fig. 3-28.

Now place the boat seat swivels on the extreme ends of part C (Fig. 3-29), and drill starter holes for the 10- ×-¾-inch screws. Drive them into place now through the holes in one plate of the boat swivel.

Turn the turntables on their faces and draw perpendicular lines through their centers. Turn the base assembly over onto the turntables and turn the free plate of one boat swivel so three of its screw slots can be seen on the sides and the end (Fig. 3-30). Line up the cross lines with these slots and mark the slot positions on the turntable. Drill starter holes and drive the screws into place (Fig. 3-31) through the boat swivel slots and into the turntable. Turn the turntable now so you can see the fourth slot and also insert a screw there. Repeat these operations for the turntable at the other end of the assembly. Figure 3-32 shows the finished assembly.

Fig. 3-29. Right: The boat seat swivels provide sturdy, turnable supports for shop projects. The 2 × 4 at right allows the lazy Susan to be used on a flat workbench or tabletop.

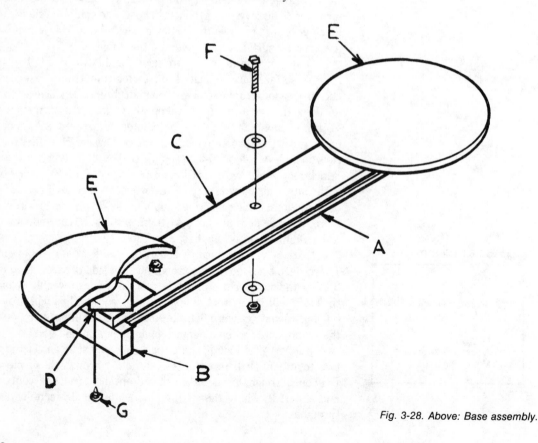

Fig. 3-28. Above: Base assembly.

147

Fig. 3-30. Notice the groove made in the 2 × 4 to provide grip for the work center. Three bolts hold it to the assembly.

Fig. 3-31. Divide each turntable into four quadrants using pencil lines. Then center the lines under the swivel slots. The turntable is actually a countertop cutout.

Fig. 3-32. The completed lazy Susan, shown upside down, is ready for use. Sturdy construction will allow use in almost any workshop project.

Fig. 3-33. Left: Hang the lazy Susan on two large nails driven partially into the wall.

The double lazy Susan is now complete. You will find it invaluable in your shop as you accomplish many intricate jobs. When you are not using it, you can easily hang it on a wall. Drive two large nails into the wall about 10 inches apart and hang it from them, with their surfaces facing the wall (see Fig. 3-33).

PROJECT 16: ROUTER GUIDES

Several projects described in this book require the use of a router. This device has become a very common tool in home workshops. If you don't have one, perhaps you should consider it as a "hintable item" for your next birthday, Father's Day or Christmas.

Like the radial-arm saw, the router's use can be multiplied several times with simple accessories. This project describes two: a narrow workpiece fixture designed to assist in making router cuts in narrow stock (Fig. 3-34), and a dado-and-groove fixture used for controlling the router for straight cuts or flat surfaces. The former, made for use with the work center, also features a commercially available dovetailing fixture. Both functions are accomplished on one platform in order to use storage space more efficiently.

Fig. 3-34. Router guides can be invaluable adjuncts to your shop. This fixture for holding narrow workpieces provides a third hand during routing, improving accuracy and saving time and nerves. Note the dovetailing kit mounted on the same fixture.

Narrow Workpiece Fixture

As with other work-center projects, the base of this one is a 29-inch-long, 2-×-4 piece. Other material needed are a 14½-×-21-inch piece of ¾-inch AC plywood, two 21-inch-long lengths of 2-×-2 stock, four small screw eyes, and six 10-gauge-1½-inch wood screws. Also see Table 3-7.

Start by placing the piece of plywood on your work surface. Lay the 2×4 across it, longways, in the center. Make a pencil mark on each side of the 2×4 to indicate its position, and then remove the 2×4. Now drill three holes through the plywood, between those pencil lines, the same diameter as the screws. Exact location isn't crucial, but be sure that the screws are far enough from all edges. Use a countersink drill to allow the screws to be driven in flush with the surface. Place the piece of plywood onto the 2-×-4 stock so that it is now in the same position it was before (except it is now *under* the plywood rather than *on* it), and drill starter holes, through the larger holes just drilled, into the 2×4. See Fig. 3-35. Drive the screws now.

Turn this assembly over on its top, with the 2×4 up, and lay one piece of 2-×-2 stock under a long edge. The other piece of 2×2 can

Table 3-7. Project 16 Tools.

Saw
Square
Countersink Bit
Router
Drill
Clamps
Measuring Tape
Pliers

Fig. 3-35. Cut your plywood base to size, then drill and countersink three screw holes to attach the 2 × 4 that will be held by the work center. The base must be wide enough to allow the edge of the attached dovetailing kit to extend over the work center edge.

Fig. 3-36. Attach the 2 × 2 on the opposite surface of the plywood base from the 2 × 4. Countersinking these holes will reduce scratching of your work center surface.

be temporarily laid under the other edge to serve as a support. Mark for three screws in the plywood stock, to be driven into the piece of 2×2, and drill and countersink as before. Apply white glue to the piece of 2×2, drive the three screws home, and tighten them. See Fig. 3-36. Turn the assembly over so that the 2×4 is again on the bottom. You might want to insert it into the work center to provide a helping hand for the rest of the operation.

Draw a light pencil line 8 inches in from the edge of the plywood that has the attached 2×2. Make a cross mark 6 inches in on this line, from each end, and turn in two screw eyes at these two points. Measure 4 inches on a centerline on the remaining 2-×-2 piece and screw in a screw eye in one of these points. Tie two 5½-inch-long rubber bands together (or their equivalent combined length), and attach one end of a band to the last (still unattached) screw eye. Thread the other end of the bands through the screw eyes driven into the plywood, and then attach the remaining, loose, screw eye to that free end.

Because you must now screw in this remaining screw eye, but you do not want the rubber bands to have a permanent twist in them, twist the bands counterclockwise about six turns before you screw this last screw eye into the piece of 2×2. To ensure an untwisted band at completion, count the returns taken into the 2×2 by the first screw eye.

Now screw the last screw eye into place. You will note that the band conveniently holds the 2×2 in place (Fig. 3-37), yet it can be moved and clamped into position when it is used (Fig. 3-38). This eliminates lost fixture pieces, and it uncomplicates your life just one step more.

To attach the dovetail kit, follow the general directions given by the manufacturer. The base of the dovetail kit used here is 1½-inches deep, the exact depth of the 2×2s, so the 2×2s actually help your use of the dovetail kit by holding the long end of the

Fig. 3-37. This is the finished assembly ready for use. Note the rubber bands that hold the moveable jig piece.

Fig. 3-38. C-clamps hold the router fixture tight against stock for accurate and speedy cutting. When the C-clamps are removed, the moveable jig piece will spring back to its "open" position.

workpiece at the proper height. Make sure the kit you use is at least this deep. If it is not, make whatever adjustments are necessary in the depth of the two 21-inch-long fixture pieces.

To use the fixture, first clamp it in your work center. Place the workpiece against the stationary rail and hold the adjustable rail firmly next to it with a C-clamp at each end. The router then slides across the top of the two rails. It is held in proper alignment by the router's guide that slides along the outer edge of the stationary rail.

You will find yourself using this fixture often, in a variety of situations, such as for routing of small stock or for dovetailing. When it is not in use, you will find it very easy to store on your tool and fixture rack (Project 11). It will conveniently "stand on end," at the back of a pair of braces, to allow another fixture to be held in front of it.

Dado and Groove Fixture

The dado and groove fixture shown in Fig. 3-39 will also be a handy addition to your routing bag of tricks. It will be particularly useful for making dadoes for shelves and other such cross-the-stock applications. But you'll find you can also use it at the end of stock for making rabbets or near-the-edge dadoes (Fig. 3-40).

Fig. 3-39. The dado and groove fixture provides an easy and accurate method for making these common cuts. Notice the dado in the end piece of the fixture; it is made as the first dado is cut.

Fig. 3-40. This fixture can also be used to cut dadoes and rabbets at the end of the stock. Be sure that the fixture is snug against the work-piece before starting the cut.

The fixture is made of two 18-inch-long pieces of stock and two 12-inch-long pieces. Stock used for the one in the illustrations was a one-half inch by 1½-inch, but you can use ¾-inch-thick stock by 2 or 3 inches if you prefer.

First drill four screw holes in each 12-inch piece, as shown in Fig. 3-41, and countersink the holes so the screws' heads will be flush with or below the surface. The distance between parts A (see Figs. 3-42 and 3-43) is the exact diameter of your router base.

Using a carpenter's square, line up part A and part B so that they are square. Clamp them together in this position. Drill starter holes through the holes in part B into A. Apply white glue between the pieces and drive in the screws. Be careful to maintain the squareness. Do the same at all four joints.

To use this fixture, place it over the workpiece so that one end piece rides along its edge. Put your router between the side pieces and move the assembly to the exact location of the groove to be made. Clamp the fixture at that location and you will be assured of a perpendicular groove. You will find this to be a very easy-to-use and helpful aid.

You can also use the fixture for nonperpendicular grooves. Simply angle the fixture properly before clamping it to the work-piece.

Fig. 3-41. Assemble the fixture with countersunk screws. Be sure it is square before drilling starter holes so that dadoes and grooves cut with it will also be square.

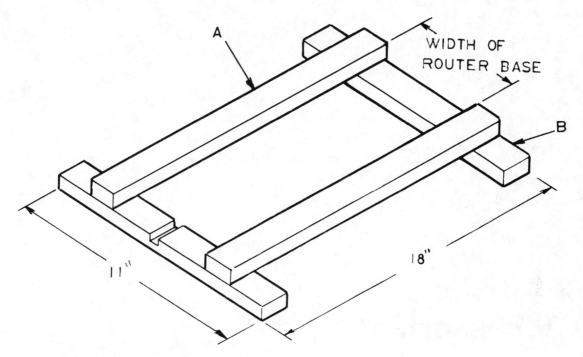

Fig. 3-42. Dado and groove fixture.

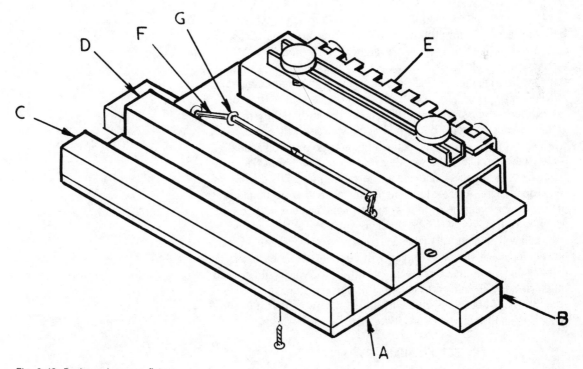

Fig. 3-43. Dado and groove fixture.

4

Accessories

N O MATTER WHAT SHOP PROJECT YOU TACKLE, INVARIABLY
the time comes when you simply don't have enough hands.
Solving that continuing problem is the basic reason for this chapter.

Some of these projects are straightforward. Bench hooks and
feather boards hold stock. Taper jigs keep stock at a preset angle as
it moves through the saw and a radial-arm saw's auxiliary table puts
stock up high enough for you to get the most use out of that tool.

Other projects are more obtuse, perhaps, but they play an
equally important role. While folding sawhorses will present the
work at a comfortable level, as the auxiliary tables do on a smaller
scale, they also make the work surface free of wobbles. The saw
guide establishes a saw line and at the same time holds the saw at
the proper angle. A water level helps you make measurements, the
picture-frame clamp holds things, and even the nail box helps out by
providing a handy way to hold the nails you need at the moment.

You will not need all of these accessories for your next project,
but before much time passes you will be able to use each one to
make your work easier or to help with work you could not do
otherwise. If you build each accessory as you see a need for it, you'll
soon have most of them built. Why not start now so that they'll be
ready for you when you're ready for them?

PROJECT 17: AUXILIARY TABLE SET

If you are just starting your shop, one of the most useful tools you can acquire is a radial-arm saw. It promotes cutting accuracy, streamlines assembly and, with proper attachments, can do jobs totally divorced from the "normal" cutting function as many define it.

The radial-arm saw is much more versatile than many users might suspect. By making proper accessory equipment, such as the set of auxiliary tables described here, you can take advantage of this versatility. The two tables can be used closely together to help you accomplish certain chores, and they can be used separately to accomplish other tasks.

Examples? Place the two tables as shown in Fig. 4-1 and you can use the saw in an adjustable horizontal position. This makes it a snap to cut grooves and rabbets in board edges. A special T-square lets you work on ends of narrow stock (Fig. 4-2).

Reverse the position of the two tables and you are ready to use your shaper and molding-head attachments. The special table surface cutout allows the blades to extend to below the surface (Fig. 4-3). The table is constructed to let you use special feather-board holddowns (see Project 18). And by using only one table, you can use a standard blade to cut deep into the end of a board (Fig. 4-4).

Fig. 4-1. The versatile pair of auxiliary tables provides a good platform for horizontal sawing when put in this position.

Fig. 4-2. This horizontal T-square makes horizontal sawing of narrow stock easy. It slides along the front edge of the table.

Fig. 4-3. When the two tables are positioned in this manner, opposite that shown in Fig. 4-1, the radial saw's molding head can be used. Notice the cutout allows the head to extend to below the surface.

Fig. 4-4. By using one table only, the radial-arm saw blade can be pulled forward to make cuts in stock ends. This feature is useful for making lap joints.

In keeping with one of the purposes of this book—to conserve shop space—you'll notice that the two auxiliary tables are designed to store "accessories' accessories." Feather boards and a T-square can be tucked neatly away beneath the tables along with a handy push stick used to push narrow stock between the blade and the fence (Fig. 4-5). The tables can be stored out of the way by using hooks that support them from a pegboard or other surface.

Cutting the Parts

Cut parts from a piece of ¾-inch AC plywood. See Fig. 4-6 and Table 4-1. Make only the *long* (48-inch) cuts now. Next, make the dado cut in the 48-inch-long part that will become "B" and "C" to assure perfect alignment of the back surface of each table. When that is completed, cut parts B and C apart and finish A, following cutting measurements shown in Fig. 4-7. Now finish part B using the same measurements in "mirror image."

C-clamp a stop onto the radial-arm saw fence 17 inches from the saw blade; use it to make identical crosscuts to separate parts B from C, D from D, and E from E. Reset the stop at 11 inches and make the four F-piece cuts. Use the scrap from the D-D strip to make four triangular gluing supports.

Table 4-1. Project 17 Tools.

Saw
Hammer
Screwdriver
Square
Countersink Bit
Drill
Clamps
Measuring Tape
Molding Blade

Because it would be hard to accurately position the separate table surface pieces A for making the molding head cutout, this cut is made before the pieces are separated. Remove the fence and clamp the 48-inch-long A-A strip to the radial-arm saw table, as shown in Fig. 4-8, with ¾-inch spacers between the table and workpiece.

Put a flat planer and jointer blade into the molding head, and install it on the saw motor. Make a pencil mark on the auxiliary table surface to indicate the planned depth of the cut. Now adjust the motor so that the molding head is in its horizontal position, with the bottom edge of the blades at ⅛ of an inch below the workpiece's top surface.

Install the guard, put on safety glasses, start the saw, and pull the motor very slowly toward you. Remove the 8-inches of stock thickness until the blade is within 1/16 of an inch of the pencil mark. Move the cutter back, lower it an eighth of an inch, and repeat the pass.

Continue until all the waste is removed. Then raise the cutter blade to just above the work surface, move it forward until the blades are even with the mark while the cutter is rotating, and *very* slowly lower the blade through the piece.

Fig. 4-5. The under side of the auxiliary tables is designed to hold feather boards, the T-square, and a push stick to provide compactness desirable in small shops.

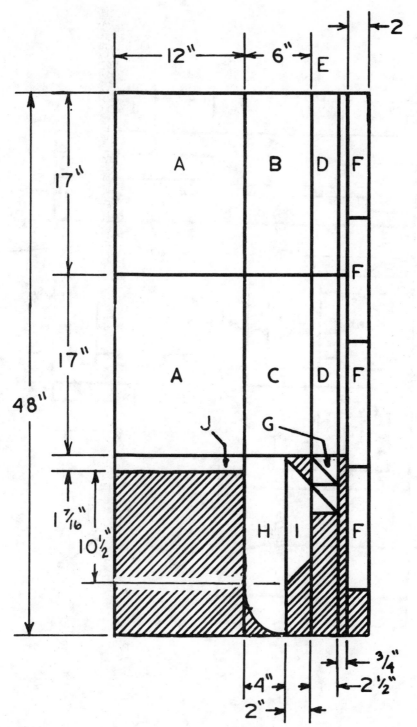

Fig. 4-6. Table cuts.

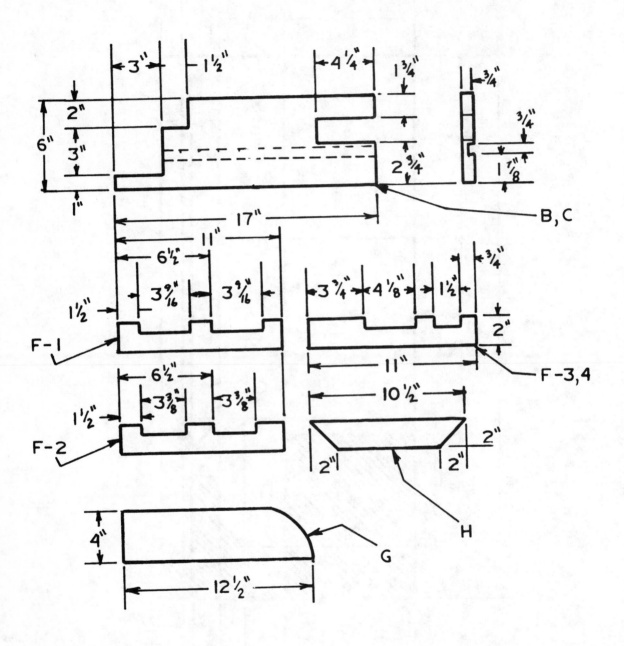

Fig. 4-7. Cutting measurements.

Fig. 4-8. Make the molding head cutout before separating table surfaces in order to promote accurate cutting.

Mark the center point on the cut arc just made, change to a standard saw blade, and cut the two "A" pieces apart. Cut off the extreme ends of the pieces to leave each of the two "A" pieces 17 inches long.

The last cutting step for the table is to finish parts F. Following the example shown in Fig. 4-7.

Fig. 4-10. Right: Use both nails and glue to make the tables. Be sure to assemble them at one setting, before the glue dries, to allow adjustments for squaring pieces for a perfect fit.

Assembling the Tables

Assembly is easy and can be done quite quickly, but take care to be as exacting as possible. A slightly crooked piece, nailed and glued permanently into place, can ruin the accuracy of the work you perform on the set of tables. Because assembly of both units is almost identical, instructions are provided on the building of one. Be sure to complete all gluing and nailing on each at one "setting" so that the total unit can be adjusted for trueness before the glue dries.

To start, put white glue on one surface of part E, carefully line it up with the edge of D (see the illustrations for positioning). After making sure one side and two ends are flush, nail four 1¼-inch finish nails along the edge through D and E.

Apply glue to the "free" edge of D (Fig. 4-9) and nail it to part

Fig 4-9. Table parts.

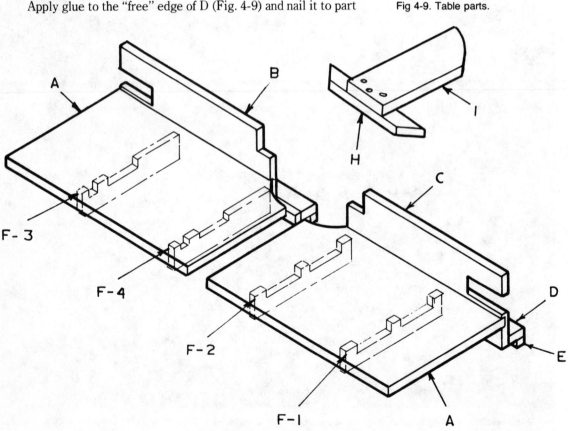

D. Now stand part A on its front edge and insert the other edge into the groove of part B, make sure the flat ends of each are flush. Glue and nail the parts into place.

Supports F1 and F2 are used with this table unit. With the table in front of you, in position with part E to the back, place F1 under the table to the right—5 inches from the right edge—and F2 3 inches from the left edge. Be sure that they are oriented correctly with each other so that feather boards can be inserted later. Note that slots in one—the left support—are slightly shorter than those in the other. This allows feather boards, when pushed in from the right side, to compress slightly in the second support and thus maintain a tight friction hold.

Apply glue and nail down through the tabletop into the top edge of the F pieces, and through the backboard piece into one end of each F piece (Fig. 4-10). The last assembly step on the tables is to glue two gussets (part G) to each in order to ensure sturdy and true units.

When you assemble the second table, be sure the F pieces are correctly oriented to accept the T-square and push stick. The T-square consists of parts H and I (Fig. 4-9). Clamp the two pieces together, using a try square, to make sure their edges are perfectly perpendicular to each other. Then drill for, countersink, and insert three screws (Fig. 4-11).

Fig. 4-11. Use a try square to make sure the T-square is accurate. Use both glue and screws to obtain an immovable joint.

Fig. 4-12. Feather boards, while relatively simple to make, perform a big job in the shop. Use them to make cutting both easier and safer.

Cut push stick J from the A-A waste and make a square-cornered cutout on its "working end" that will later hook over workpieces being cut on the tables. Although its actual shape is not crucial, give it a slight tilt for working comfort.

Your do-all auxiliary table set is now complete. You will find it will solve many problems for you in the coming years and multiply the value of your radial-arm saw many times over.

PROJECT 18: FEATHER BOARDS

If someone were to redesign the average home craftsman, they undoubtedly would provide him with a third hand. Many of the projects in this book are simply man-made solutions to this seemingly constant shortage. The feather boards shown in Fig. 4-12 provide a third hand that at times is invaluable when working with a radial-arm saw or a circular saw. Two hands are needed to properly guide a piece through the saw, but you must somehow also hold the piece in its proper relationship to the molding head or other accessory. In some instances, even if you did have three hands, it would be dangerous to use them. Feather boards are frequently used to provide safety in situations that might otherwise lead to a kickback or an unpredictable cut.

Fig. 4-13. Feather boards can be clamped into position at a variety of angles to hold work stock against the fence for accurate cutting. They are helpful on the standard sawing table and on auxiliary tables, as shown in Project 17.

The feather board shown in Fig. 4-13 is made from a piece of 1-×-4-inch fir stock. Its width is 3½ inches (see Fig. 4-14). That is the same dimension used in the radial-arm saw auxiliary table (Project 17) that stores it. If you do not plan to make the set of auxiliary tables, neither the feather board's length nor the width is a crucial dimension. See Table 4-2.

To make the feather board on your radial-arm saw, first make a jig from a piece of 2×4 (as shown in Fig. 4-15). Drive two nails through it so that their points extend a quarter to half an inch beyond the surface. Press the flat side of your workpiece onto these nails; use a hammer to force it flat against the 2×4. This will provide a sturdy support and hold the workpiece up to where the saw blade can cut between the "feathers" without leaving a long, uncut portion on the underside. Make a pencil mark across the piece to signal the ends of the feather cuts.

With a ruler, measure off and mark the width of the "feathers" at the workpiece end. Set the saw blade guard so that its front almost touches the top of this workpiece (Fig. 4-16), turn the saw on, and slowly feed it into the saw until the blade touches the pencil mark. Repeat this procedure at each of the end marks until all feathers have been made.

One edge of the feather board should be rounded (Fig. 4-12) so that this accessory need not be clamped in a specific angle each time it is used. Either make a freehand drawing of this curve with a pencil or use an artist's French curve; then cut along this line. Sand this

Table 4-2. Project 18 Tools.

Saw
Hammer
Clamps
Measuring Tape

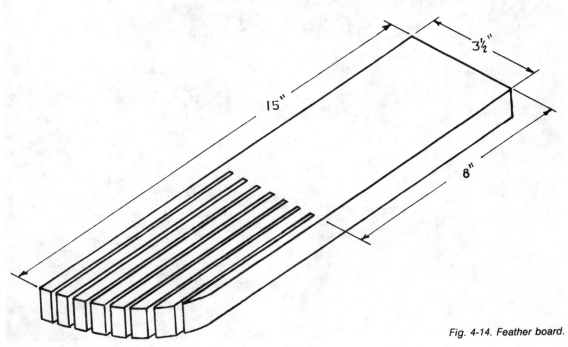

Fig. 4-14. Feather board.

edge to provide a smooth surface that will later ride on other workpieces.

The feather boards are held in position on the saw table or auxiliary table with C-clamps. To position them properly, put your workpiece on the surface as if you were about to feed it into the saw. Lay one feather board on the work surface, in a horizontal position, at an angle as shown in Fig. 4-13. Loosely attach it to the table surface with a C-clamp. Then twist the feather board toward the workpiece; force it until proper tension has been applied. Note that the tension is constantly variable, and it will increase as you continue to move the feather board. Select a position that will hold the workpiece in place, yet will allow it to be pushed through the saw. Attach the second feather board vertically to the fence and adjust it for tension in a similar manner.

Make it a habit of using the feather boards if there is even the slightest question of the need for safety. You will often find that their use enhances accuracy, provides a better looking product, and makes your time spent in the workshop just a bit more enjoyable.

PROJECT 19: VARIABLE-TAPER JIG

As you thumb through the pages of this book, you might notice references to tapering pieces of wood stock used to complete a

Fig. 4-15. Make a simple cutting jig with a 2 × 4. Drive two nails up from the bottom, and then press the work stock onto it.

Fig. 4-16. Push the cutting jig and work stock slowly into the circular-saw blade. Make sure the saw guard is positioned next to the workpiece.

Table 4-3. Project 19 Tools.

Saw
Hammer
Router
Drill
Clamps
Measuring Tape
Pliers

project. Cutting angles in wood is a fairly common operation.

Although it is possible to measure for and mark a diagonal line for cutting, an easier way is to use a variable-tapering jig (Fig. 4-17). With it, you can handle a multitude of cutting jobs almost as quickly as you can turn a wing nut.

As you can see in Fig. 4-18, the jig is easy to make. Also see Table 4-3. All that is required is two 30-inch-long pieces of ¾-inch-thick lumber (any width from 1¾ inches to perhaps 3 inches) for parts A and B, a 4-inch-long piece for part C, a 1½-inch hinge (part D), a gutter spike or another rod of similar diameter (part E), a washer (part H), and a two-ended fastener with machine threads on one end and wood threads on the other. The latter is often used to attach screw-in furniture legs into brackets.

Clamp A and B together, with their ends even, and attach the hinge to one end of the pair (see Fig. 4-19). Nail and glue part C to part B as shown in the illustrations.

Drill a hole, 2 inches from the free end of part B, to receive the gutter spike or rod. Bend the spike to form a 90-degree angle about an inch from the pointed end. Because the bend does have a radius, and the nail is to be no higher than the surface of parts B and A, rout

175

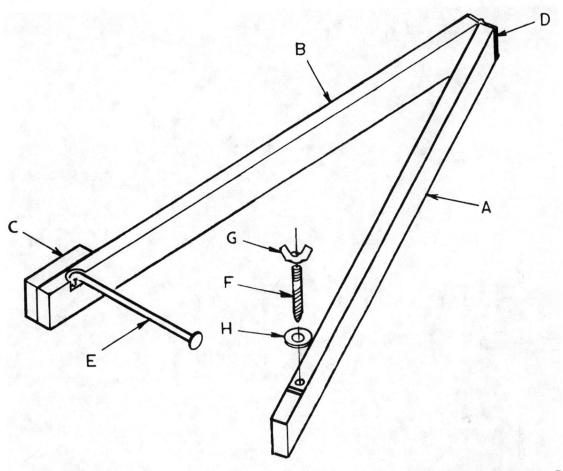

Fig. 4-18. Variable-taper jig details.

Fig. 4-17. Left: The 2 × 4 at right was cut with a radial arm saw, using the taper jig pictured. It can be adjusted to make a wide range of angles.

out a one-quarter inch or more of the area around the hole in part B so that the spike will seat itself properly (see Fig. 4-20). With that done, cut a one-eighth-inch deep groove in part A (in which the spike will rest). Notice that the top side of this spike is to remain above the surface of part A.

Drill a hole in the center of part A (as shown in Fig. 4-20) next to this groove to receive the wood-screw end of the special screw. The hole must be slightly smaller than the threads. To insert this screw, thread the wing nut onto the machine-screw end and apply a pair of pliers to it to turn the wood-screw end into part A into the wood. When it is properly seated, remove the wing nut, put the washer in place, and replace the wing nut. Tighten it down until it holds the spike securely in its selected position. See Fig. 4-21.

The last step is to make a pencil mark 12 inches from the hinge end on both parts A and B. This will be your quick-reference point for making adjustments for any plans calling for taper in inches-per-foot. To set the jig for cutting a taper that is 1 inch per foot,

Fig. 4-20. The relative position of the rod and screw holes. The screw is designed with machine threads on one end, and wood threads on the other, and is commonly used in modular furniture.

Fig. 4-19. Left: Put parts A and B together as shown, and attach the 1½-inch hinge. Be sure the pieces are flush.

measure 1 inch between parts A and B at this pencil mark (Fig. 4-22). A 2-inch-per-foot taper would require 2 inches between the pencil marks, and so on.

The jig is used by sliding side B along the fence of your radial-arm saw or circular saw. The piece to be cut rests along the length of the other leg, and is pushed through the saw by part C (Fig. 4-23).

You will find this jig to be an important tool in your arsenal of accessories. Keep it handy by your saw or in your accessory rack and you'll find more and more uses for it. You will probably wonder how you have done without it for so long.

PROJECT 20: BENCH HOOK AND MITER

For all its versatility, the radial-arm saw cannot and should not be called upon to do all of your cutting. A particularly good example is the cutting of small pieces for crafts projects, small, intricate picture frames, and other such items that could be splintered by a whirring circular saw.

A bench hook and miter combines two time-honored workbench aids: a bench hook, of similar configuration to a miter block

Fig. 4-21. Attach the washer and wing nut and tighten to hold the rod. A gutter spike was used here.

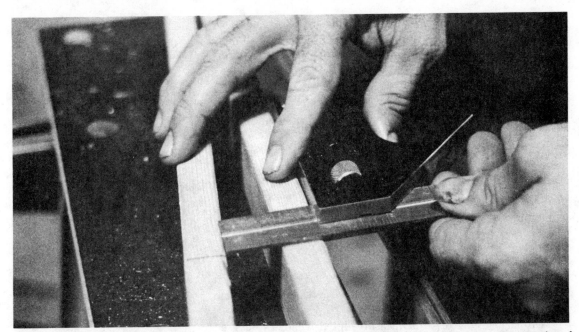

Fig. 4-22. Make a pencil mark on both legs of the jig, 12 inches from the hinged end. This will allow easy measuring of inch-to-foot tapers.

Fig. 4-23. To use the taper jig, put the work stock in place and push the jig through the saw.

except for the 45-degree cuts, and a miter block. By making these miter cuts in both parts B (Fig. 4-24), you will produce a two-in-one jig that saves space and doubles the life experienced with one-sided miter blocks. For both applications, the device is hooked over the workbench edge as shown in Fig. 4-25. One part B lodges the device tightly against the workbench top while the other part B provides both a back support against which to work and accurate miter slots for hand cutting.

This combination bench hook and miter will take on many of those small jobs that are beyond the practical limitations of the big saw. It will help you make accurate mitered-corner cuts with a tenon saw, and it will help you hold small stock for general cutting. You'll find additional uses for it as you perform multitudes of chores at the bench. It will help hold items while you drive screws into them, for example, and it will readily serve as a stop for holding other in-progress work.

To construct the bench hook and miter, cut the 8-×-10-inch base (part A) from a piece of scrap ¾-inch AC plywood. At the same time, cut the two part Bs, as shown in Fig. 4-26. Also see Table 4-4.

On one long edge of part B, measure for the eventual 45-degree cuts and, using a try square, mark their exact location. Now mark

Table 4-4. Project 20 Tools.

Saw
Screwdriver
Square
Countersink Bit
Drill
Measuring Tape

Fig. 4-24. Bench hook and miter.

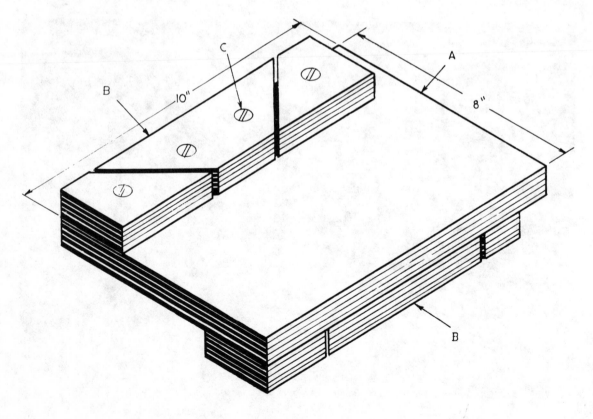

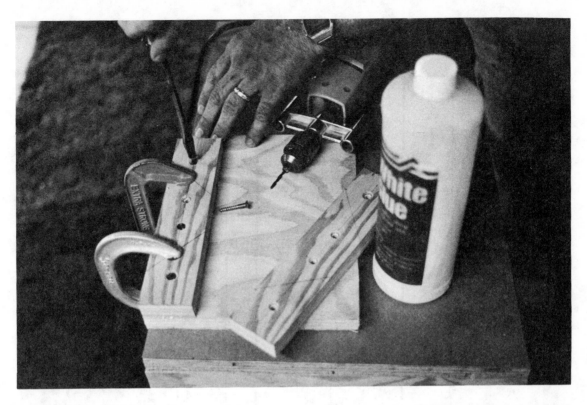

Fig. 4-25. Bench hooks and miter
blocks are invaluable workbench
accessories. This device combines
their functions to provide accurate
cutting while doubling miter block
life.

the position of the four screw holes. Drill them so that the screws
will push into them in a snug fit. Use a countersink drill bit on the
holes so that the screws will later tighten in flush.

Following placement shown in Fig. 4-24, apply glue to the
bottom of one part G and clamp it into position on part A (Fig. 4-27).
Be sure the back edges of A and B are flush with each other. Now
drill starter holes through the holes in part B into part A. Use a bit
two or three sizes smaller than the one used to make the part B
holes. Insert screw C into each of these four holes and tighten them
down.

Attach the other part B in a similar manner (noting its position
in Fig. 4-24). One end of both parts B is flush with the same edge of
part A. No matter which part B is on top, its short end is to the right.
The space it provides at the end of part A allows you to use the end
as a 90-degree cutting edge while providing a "ledge" upon which
the to-be-removed work stock can rest.

Cut the 45-degree angles next. If you have access to an accurate radial-arm saw with a thin plywood-cutting blade, use it in its
45-degree miter position to cut these slots by placing ¾-inch spacers under the back edge to make the unit level. If no such saw is
available, carefully make the cut with your tenon saw. Remember
that the miter block will only be as accurate as you are.

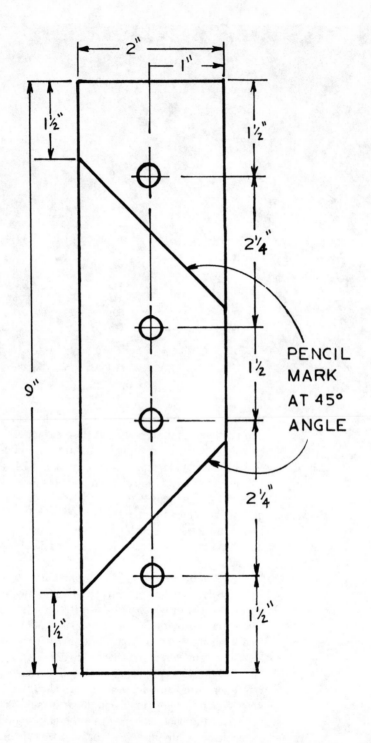

2"

1"

1½"

1½"

2¼"

9"

1½"

PENCIL
MARK
AT 45°
ANGLE

1½

2¼"

1½"

Fig. 4-26. Bench hook and miter cuts.

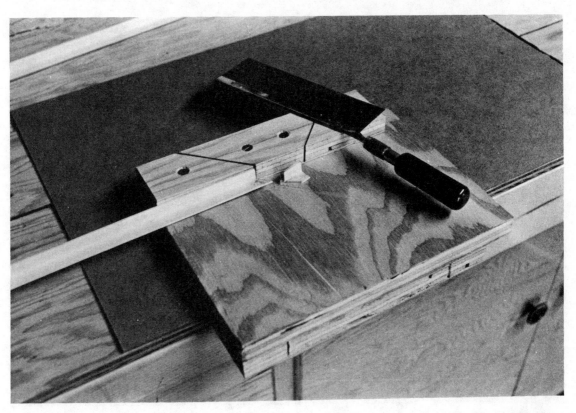

Fig. 4-27. Attach parts B before making 45-degree saw kerfs. Countersink screws; glue before tightening them in.

Your bench hook and meter is now complete. If you prefer, put screw eyes in the back so that it can be hung on a pegboard or nail. Keep it handy where you will occasionally see it. You'll soon find yourself using it for many projects.

PROJECT 21: WOBBLE-FREE, FOLDAWAY SAWHORSE

Just how often do you really need a sawhorse? Except for certain flurries of activity, the answer is probably very seldom. A good sawhorse is certainly vital at times, but between those times it is difficult to store.

The sawhorse described in this section is designed to solve that storage problem, yet provide a presto-it's-here solution when it is needed. It folds up neatly in two pieces, and it is designed to be easily stackable on the work-center accessory storage unit (Project 11). When you need the sawhorse you simply open the two pieces like jackknives, put them together, and there you have it. And if you make the sawhorse as tall as your work center, you can use the center as the *other* sawhorse and eliminate building one sawhorse.

An unusual feature of this sawhorse is its three-legged stance (Fig. 4-28). If you'll recall the last time you used a traditional sawhorse, you'll immediately recognize a disadvantage. You proba-

bly had a hard time finding a perfectly level spot on which to place it and it probably had a certain amount of inherent wobble with which you had to contend. Properly constructed and assembled, this three-legged version simply cannot wobble regardless of the terrain on which it rests.

Perhaps the best part about this sawhorse is its simplicity of construction. All you need is a 9-foot 2×4, a 4-foot-long, 7-inch-wide piece of ¾-inch plywood, two carriage bolts with washers and nuts, and a handful of nails. See Table 4-5.

Start by cutting the wood pieces as shown in Fig. 4-29. Note in Figs. 4-29 and 4-30 that most of the angles have been kept the same. This makes your cutting job easy. The reverse-angle cuts between C and D, and at the left end of part I, are easily made by flipping the stock over. The one exception to this same-angle format is found on parts J and K (see Fig. 4-30).

Assemble the one-legged end first. Lay part I (the top of the sawhorse) on the floor; place the short edge at the top. Now lay leg L against it, so that an end surface is against the bottom edge of part I, and the long outer edge of L is lined up with the left end of I (see Fig. 4-31). Put part A on top, as shown, with its top edge a half inch below part I's top edge; position its left side flush with the end of I and the

Fig. 4-28. These three-legged sawhorses will rest sturdily on any terrain, without wobble. When they are not needed, they can simply be folded up and put out of the way.

Table 4-5. Project 21 Tools.

Saw
Hammer
Screwdriver
Drill
Measuring Tape

edge of L. Drive five or six nails through A and L *only*. Do *not* put nails through part I.

Temporarily remove part I and turn the AL assembly over. Place part B on top of this assembly so that it lines up with its mate (part A). Drive nail five or six nails through it. Then turn the assembly over once again. Slip I into position at the top of L, between A and B, and make sure it fits properly in every respect. Determine the location of the pivot bolt hole by referring to Fig. 4-32 and, after checking positions once again, drill a ⅜-inch hole through the whole assembly: parts A, I, and B (Fig. 4-33). Insert the bolt and tighten it so that there is no play. The joint must be sufficiently loose enough so that the unit can be folded and opened at will.

The two-legged end is next. Lay part J on the floor, with the sliced-off side to the right, and make a pencil mark on it as shown in Fig. 4-28. Place part C on this board and a piece of scrap 2×4 so that the top is parallel to and touches that mark, and the left edge is parallel with the left edge of J. Nail in place with five nails. Turn the assembly over and nail on part D in a like manner (Fig. 4-34) so that they are in identical position on opposite sides of J.

Make a pencil mark on K, as you did on J, and insert K between

Fig. 4-29. The sawhorse is made from four pieces of 2 × 4 and a strip of plywood. A few nails, two carriage bolts with washers and nuts, and a drop-leaf hinge (not shown) complete the materials list.

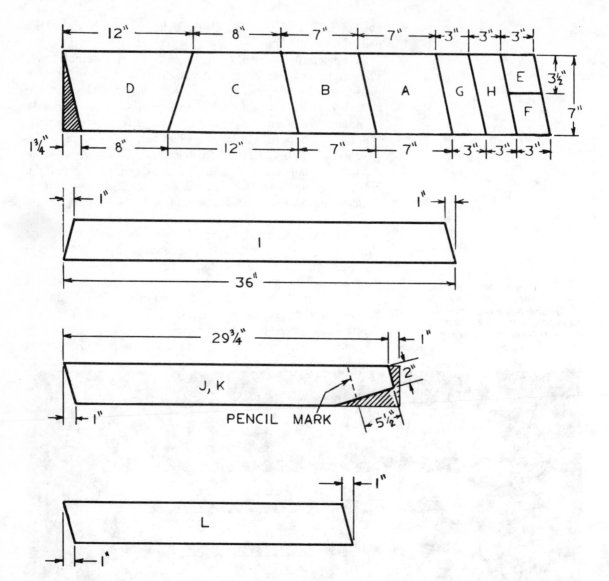

Fig. 4-30. Sawhorse parts.

C and D. Slide K up or down until that mark is even with the top edge of C, and K's right edge is flush with the right edge of C. Referring to Fig. 4-32, drill the pivot hole and insert the bolt. Tighten it as you did the first one.

Nail parts E and F to opposite sides of the end of I so that their slanted ends and their bottom edges are flush. This will leave a half-inch clearance between the parts and the top edge of part I.

On one side of part I, hold a scrap piece of 2×4 against the piece just attached and position part G next to it (see Fig. 4-35). The 2×4 acts as a spacer; it identifies the space that will later be occupied by the two-legged assembly. When you have determined that spacing

Fig. 4-31. The single leg is first assembled with its plywood pieces (A and B). The sawhorse cross piece at left (part I) is used here for positioning only; it is not nailed to the plywood.

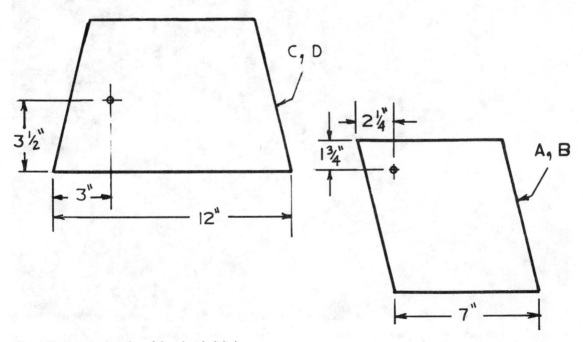

Fig. 4-32. Note the location of the pivot-bolt hole.

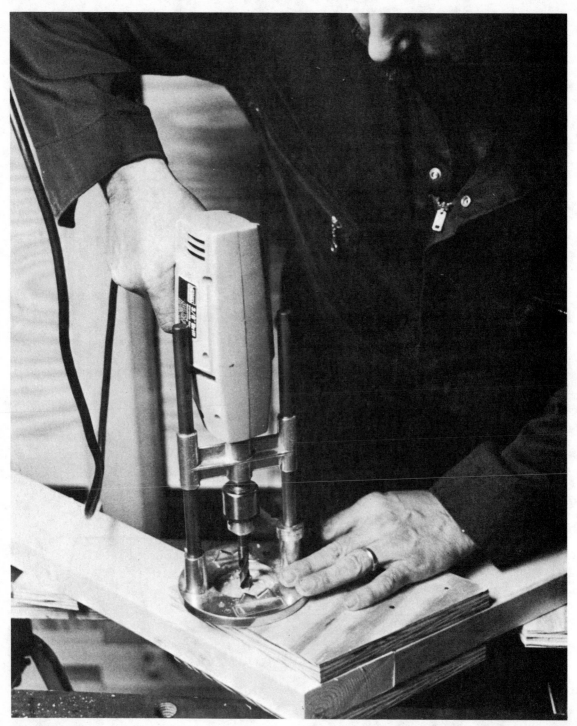

Fig. 4-33. With the cross piece I placed carefully in position, drill a 1/3-inch hole through A, I, and B. Follow the positioning shown in Fig. 4-32.

Fig. 4-34. Assemble part J with parts C and D. Note that the other leg, part K, will not be nailed into place. It will be held in place with the carriage bolt so that the pair will provide a pinch action on the cross piece.

Fig. 4-35. Use a scrap 2- ×-4 piece to provide spacing for two-legged assembly. An edge of parts E and H is flush with the bottom edge of the sawhorse cross piece to allow clearance for work pieces on the top edge.

(it should not have "play" in it, but it should allow the 2×4 to easily slip in and out), nail part G in place. Turn the assembly over and repeat the process on that side.

The construction is now almost complete. Open the two assemblies, slip them together, and set the horse on the floor. Hold it down with your hands and lightly kick the two legs outward, away from each other, to tighten their scissorslike grip against the cross member. Attach a drop leaf hinge to these legs (slightly opened as shown in Fig. 4-36). When you push the hinge down with your foot to lock it, the legs will pinch the cross piece with sufficient force to lock it tight.

To store the sawhorse, simply open the hinge and separate the two pieces. Then fold and stack them, one on the other, on the work center tool storage rack. Your workshop floor should be clear now for projects that don't require sawhorses.

PROJECT 22: PROBLEM-SOLVING WATER LEVEL

Will you ever have need to, for example, make sure a bathroom closet shelf is exactly level with your front doorbell? Of course you won't. But you *will* on occasion need to know if and when two distant

Fig. 4-36. Note the open position of the hinge when the other ends of the two legs are in contact with the sawhorse cross piece. When the hinge is straightened, the assembly will pinch the cross piece in order to provide a tight mating.

Table 4-6. Materials List for a Problem-Solving Water Level.

1″ × 2″ × 7′ fir, clear (actual 11/16″ × 1½″)	4
½″ male hose coupling	2
½″ female hose coupling	2
3/8 I.D., 9/16 O.D. clear plastic hose, 6′ long	2
yardsticks	8
3-penny nails	As needed
Glue	As needed
Rubber bands	2

points are level. The traditional methods will not always work well. Consider these rather common examples:

☐ You want to hang cabinets, on one wall, at the same level as those on the opposite wall or in another room.

☐ You want to pour a level building foundation at the same height as another building's foundation.

☐ You want to determine the slope of your yard.

☐ You want to install a level fence.

This list could go on indefinitely, but the point should be apparent. Every homeowner occasionally needs an easy, accurate, and flexible leveling system. Ideally, it will provide a useful reference point for a whole area, but it must cost only a few dollars.

Is there such a device? Yes, and you can make it easily in your own shop. See Fig. 4-37. It requires only a length of hose, couplings, yardsticks, nails, and a few feet of 1-×-2 lumber. See Tables 4-6 and 4-7. It is a simple project to make. When you have completed it, you will have a tool that will streamline a lifetime of building and landscaping efforts.

How the Water Level Works

First a quick word about how the water level works. Perhaps every adult has heard the saying, "water seeks its own level," but many don't know just what that means. In plain terms, it means that all surfaces of water in an open container will remain level even if that vessel has odd-shaped, open-topped tubes or other appurtenences into which the fluid has moved.

For a simple illustration of this principal, fill a clear plastic hose half full with water, and then bend it into a U-shape with its ends pointed upward. The water surface in one tube will be level with that in the other. If you raise or lower one leg of that "U," the water surfaces in the legs will remain level with each other until the water eventually pours out of the short leg.

The water level project described here is just such a U-shaped hose, but with refinements added. Each of two identical units represent one leg of that "U." The bottom of each tube is fitted with a

Table 4-7. Project 22 Tools.

Saw
Hammer
Measuring Tape

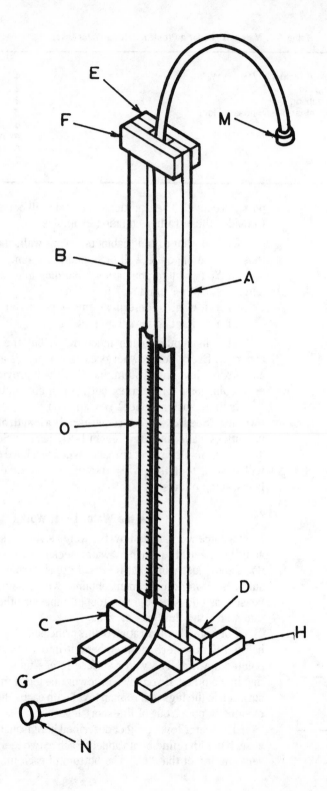

Fig. 4-37. The level parts.

standard garden-hose fitting—one male, and the other female—and could be attached to complete the "U." By introducing a garden hose between them, you have the capability of leveling points a great distance away.

Notice that each unit also has a pointer, that crosses perpendicular to the hose, and a pair of attached yardsticks. Because the two units are exactly identical, the water level reading of one will be the same as that of the other if the two units are sitting on points that are exactly level with each other. If one unit shows a 26-inch reading, as an example, and the other shows only a 24-inch reading, that would mean the second unit is sitting on a surface 2 inches higher than the first. Such information can be used several ways to solve a variety of measuring problems.

Constructing the Water Level

Cut all wooden parts, as shown in Fig. 4-37 for both level units. It is particularly important that parts A and B (for both) be identical in length, that they be assembled with their mating parts in an identical manner, and that the four yardsticks—that both retain the tubing and provide the comparative readings—be positioned exactly. See Fig. 4-38.

Assemble parts A, B, C, D, and E as shown in Fig. 4-39. Be sure that parts A and B are perpendicular to the other pieces. If they are not, the finished unit might either lean to one side or the two yardsticks on each side might be slightly uneven—thus making the level inaccurate.

The top edges of parts A and B should be flush with the ends of part E (leaving proper spacing for the hose). Make sure that the bottoms of A and B are the same distance apart as the tops (3½ inches), and center them at the spacing between parts C and D. They should extend *beyond* C and D no more than the depth of parts G and H or the finished unit might wobble. Before nailing A, B, C, and D in place, use G and H to check positions carefully.

Cut two 6-foot lengths of clear plastic hose and attach a male and a female "replacement" fitting at each end of each piece (Fig. 4-40). Crimp their metal fingers tightly into the hose by using a pair of pliers.

Lay one hose into the cradle, formed by parts A and B (Fig. 4-41), with approximately the same amount of tubing extending at each end. The male fitting should be at the top of one unit and at the bottom of the other. Notice that there is a snug fit between the hose and the upright members. This helps hold the hose straight along the length of parts A and B. Now nail part F into place.

With the partial assembly still in its flat position, nail two yardsticks to each side, as shown in the photos, overlapping the inside edges of A and B by an ⅛ of an inch. Make sure the top of each

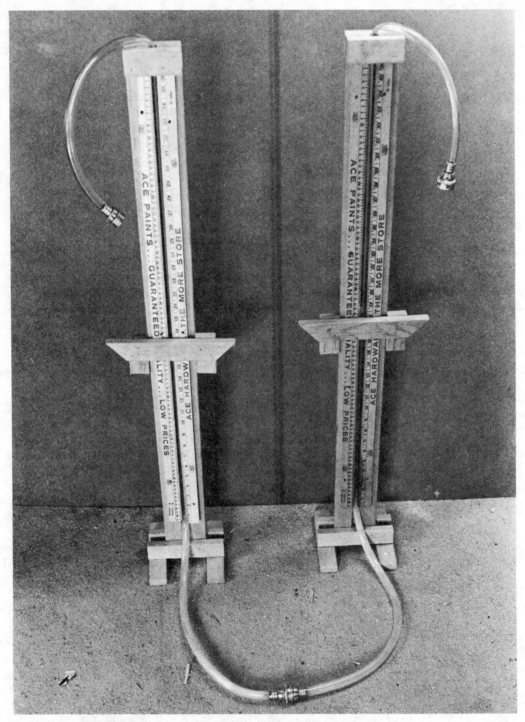

Fig. 4-38. This set of water levels is simple to make, yet can solve significant problems for you. In use, a long length of hose separates them.

Fig. 4-39. Make sure all parts are assembled correctly by using a square. Mistakes here can be repeated in your finished project.

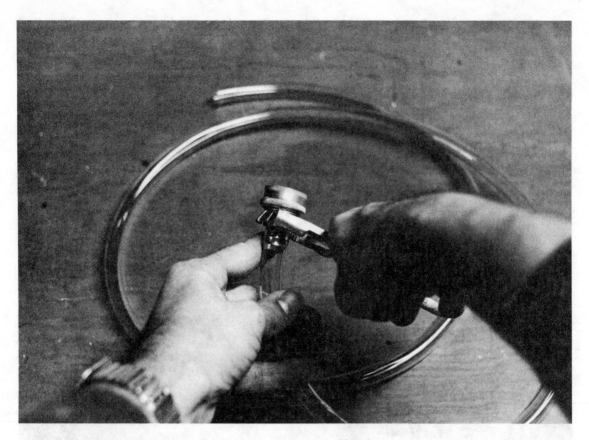

yardstick touches part F and that the measurement scales are facing each other, next to the tube. Notice that this positioning leaves ample room for the hose to exit between the bottom of the yardsticks and part C. If you use "inches" on one side and "centimeters" on the other, as was done in this example, you will have both the advantages of measuring differences in inches and making fine-line adjustments in centimeters.

The pointer is next. Cut the pieces as shown in Fig. 4-42. The insides of parts J and K are long in order to ensure that the completed pointer remains perpendicular to the unit's upright members. Drive nails into the outside edge of each of these pieces as shown, about three-fourths of an inch down, to eventually retain the rubber band that will help hold the completed pointer in position.

Lay part I across uprights A and B, determine that it is square (use a carpenter's square), and position J and K beneath its ends. Nail and glue the components together so that the completed assembly will slide up and down, yet it will be somewhat held in place by friction. To complete the water level, attach the pointers to the main unit with rubber bands.

Fig. 4-40. Attach a male replacement connection to one end of the hose and a female connection to the other. Clear hose is needed so that you can see the water level.

Fig. 4-41. Right: Insert the hose between the two side pieces before attaching them at the top. A male connection is to exit out the bottom of one unit and a female is to exit out of the bottom of the other. The yardsticks, when in place on both sides of the unit, help to hold the hoses in place.

198

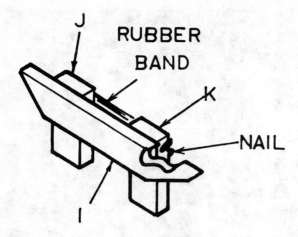

J

RUBBER BAND

K

NAIL

I

Fig. 4-42. Pointer cuts.

Testing the Level

It is now time to test your level. Connect the two bottom hose ends; tighten them down with pliers to eliminate any possibility of leaks. You can, if you like, use a garden hose for the test. But be sure the gaskets are good and the connections are airtight. Any leaks at all will soon take the water level down below the yardstick scales.

Now connect the top male end to a water source and run water through the system until all air is driven out. Disconnect the hose from this water source and stand the two units next to each other on a level surface. Observe the water surface in each. If it is too high, turn one unit on its side and let some water flow out until the level falls to about halfway down the yardstick scales.

Move each pointer to where its top surface is exactly level with the water line, and then set the two units next to each other on a level surface. If they have been constructed properly, the pointers should be exactly level with each other. If there is a slight difference, the yardsticks on one unit can be moved down slightly to compensate. Be sure the fault is with the level and not with the surface on which the two units rest. To find out, switch the positions of the two units. If each then has the same reading as it had before, the units must be adjusted. If they have reversed their readings, the surface is not level and you have thus completed your first level measurement.

Using Your Water Level

The level set can be used in many different ways to solve many different problems. The following are some typical applications; you're sure to think of more.

Leveling Lines on Separate Walls. Let's assume you want to have that bathroom closet shelf exactly level with your front doorbell, or more likely, a planned row of wall cabinets on one wall to be level with an existing row on the opposite wall or in another room.

Put one level unit (unit A) next to the wall that has the cabinets already in place and the other unit (unit B) next to the other wall. Move unit A's pointer to its water level line, and turn the unit so that the pointer touches the wall. Measure from that point (up to the cabinets).

Now adjust unit B's pointer to its water level line and measure the same distance up the wall as you measured at unit A. You have now determined the new cabinet's height. Move unit B to another position along the wall and make both unit A and B measurements again (Remember that the floor might not be level and therefore unit A's level might change. Mark as before. A line drawn across those two points is level with the cabinets in the other room.

Setting Forms for a Level Foundation. Let's assume you plan to pour a garage foundation several yards away from your house and you want to be level with a given line on the house foundation. Set level unit A next to the house and unit B at a corner of the planned garage. Move unit A's pointer to the house foundation line and measure the distance between it and the water level. Now observe unit B's water level and add (or subtract) the distance measured at unit A to determine where unit B's pointer should be. Mark that point on a stake.

Make similar measurements for the other three corners. Remember each time to remeasure the water-level-to-line distance at the house. It will have changed as the yard level itself changes from corner to corner. The plane represented by those four corner-stake points will be level and at the same height as the reference point on the wall.

Determining the Slope of Your Yard. Let's assume that, for drainage purpose or whatever, you want to know the slope of your yard. Set Unit A at one point and Unit B 25 ft. away. Read the water level line measure point at both units and multiply the difference between the two readings by four. If your measurement at Unit A is, say, an inch longer than the one at Unit B, your slope is four inches per 100 ft.

Installing a Level Fence. Let's assume that you want to put in a level fence on rolling ground. Position each of the units at an end post. If it is a low fence or if you need a level line for a strand of wire to start from a known position at unit A, put the unit A pointer at that spot on the post, note the distance from it to the level line, and put unit B's pointer at that same distance from its own water level line. You can now sight from pointer to pointer along the fence and you can guide an assistant who is doing the actual stapling, nailing, or marking at the posts between the end ones.

If your fence or nailing line is taller than these units, set unit

A's pointer at its level line, next to the end post, and measure up to the already known starting point. Measure up that same distance from unit B's level line, which is positioned at the post at the other end of the planned fence, and put a second nail there. Sighting along these nails will provide a level line.

These are only examples of possible uses for your new set of water levels. They can also be used, in a very simple manner, to determine a very simple line on one wall. Even if this is the only use you have for a leveling system at the moment, the effort you will put into making the level will more than pay for itself. It's almost guaranteed that one day soon you will have more exotic problems to solve with the levels.

PROJECT 23: MEASURING FENCE AND STOP

One of the most important functions you perform in your shop is the measurement of components that will later be assembled into a project. Careless measurements will lead to sloppy construction and the results will look amateurish to say the least.

This project combines sawing and measuring functions by putting the measurement directly onto the radial-arm saw's fence. This eliminates the measurement step that requires making a pencil mark on the workpiece. Elimination of such middle steps can lead to more accurate cutting. This assumes that the measuring device itself is accurate.

This project goes one step further by also providing a cut-off stop to be used in the measuring process. If you have 10 pieces to cut the same length, you need only place this stop at the proper point on the fence and hold the workpiece against it while cutting the 10 individual pieces. They will be identical in length, save you cutting time, and, again, enhance accuracy.

Central to the measurement fence is an aluminum yardstick. As you'll note in Fig. 4-43A. The yardstick has been cut into two pieces, and its two original ends are flush with the edge of the saw's cut through the fence. The yardstick used here has measuring marks on both edges. This eliminates mental gymnastics to determine a length. As an example, a piece of stock can be cut to 7 inches on either side of the blade, and the stop itself can be used on either side. On the saw shown in the illustrations, the stop can be used no closer than 10 inches on the right-hand side because of the saw's motor (Fig. 4-43B). Thus any cuts shorter than that are made on the left side (Fig. 4-44).

Constructing the Fence

Making the fence is a rather simple operation. See Table 4-8. Its length will, of course, be the width of your saw table (in this case, 3 feet), and the fence's height will be the width of the yardstick plus

Fig. 4-43A. Attaching a yardstick to your fence saves measuring time and it can increase accuracy. This aluminum yardstick is attached with countersunk screws to allow clearance of wood stock.

Table 4-8. Project 23 Tools.

Saw
Hammer
Screwdriver
Countersink Bit
Router
Drill
Clamps
Measuring Tape

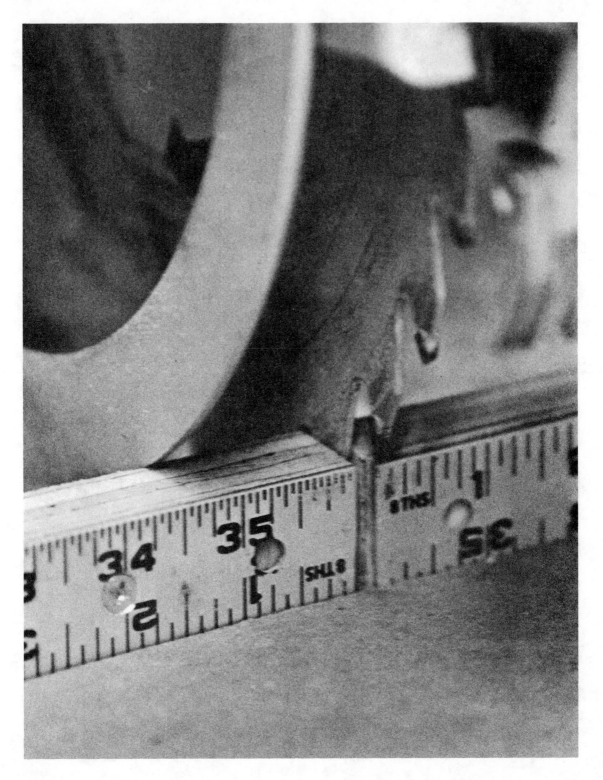

Fig. 4-44. The stop can be used on either the right or left side of the blade to provide versatility in cutting.

Fig. 4-43B. Left: The stop, squeezed onto the fence by action of a compressed rubber ball, provides an easy way to make repeat cuts.

the depth of the table from its surface to the substructure on which it is mounted. Stock varying from ¾ of an inch to 1 inch is often used as a table surface. If you have applied an additional layer above this to take the punishment of the saw blade, as many craftsmen do, you must take this into consideration.

Insert this fence into its position in your saw table, making sure that the ends are flush with the edges of the table, and tighten it into position. Clamp the yardstick into position on its face and, very slowly, pull the saw through the fence-yardstick assembly, with the blade set a fraction of an inch below the table surface. You will notice that when the two severed pieces of yardstick are turned upside down (still facing you) and held against the fence, each will measure from zero at the saw blade.

The pieces are to be attached to the fence with 6-gauge, ⅜-inch wood screws. Clamp each piece of yardstick to a waste piece of wood and drill ⅜-inch holes through each piece. The holes in the unit illustrated are at 2, 7, and 12 inches on the short piece, and 3, 11, and 19 inches on the long one. Use your countersink drill to ream these holes so that the screws' heads will be flush with the yardstick's surface.

Now reposition the pieces onto the fence itself, being careful to make them flush with the sawmark just cut, and clamp them tightly into place. Drill starter holes at the center of each hole into the fence (or use a small nail) and drive the six screws home. The fence is complete and may be used now. Make the proper mitered cuts if you prefer. This will require adding countersunk screws at each side of each cut.

Making the Stop

In a way, the stop resembles a spring-loaded clothes pin, and it functions in a similar manner. It is easy to make and it requires only two small pieces of scrap plywood, a loose-in hinge, a rubber ball such as is found in a child's "jacks" game, two rubber bands, and a couple of brads.

Start by cutting the wood pieces from ¾-inch AC plywood. You might want to leave the pieces intact until after they have been rabbetted and routed (as shown in Fig. 4-45). A chamfering bit is used to make the depressions that will help hold the rubber ball into place.

Separate the leaves of the hinge and screw them into place as shown in Fig. 4-46. The bottom edge of each should be flush with the

Fig. 4-45. Cut the two pieces of the stop from a scrap piece of plywood. This one was made with parts still attached in order to facilitate cutting and routing.

Fig. 4-46. Separate a loose-pin hinge's leaves and attach them to the stop's legs. The depression for the rubber ball was made with a router bit.

edge of the rabbet. Next, put a small brad into the center of the ends opposite the rabbets.

To assemble, hold the pieces together so that the hinge leaves intermesh and put the pin through the hinge. Place the rubber ball between the two plywood pieces so that it seats in the routed-out depression. Squeeze the assembly as you tightly wrap a rubber band around the two brads (see Fig. 4-47). You will note that the rubber ball applies a constant force that pinches this assembly to the fence. The rubber band applies a lesser force that keeps the rubber ball locked into place when the stop is not in use. To increase the hold of the stop on the fence, wrap another rubber band around the rabbeted portion of the back leg of the assembly. Increased friction between it and the fence will substantially reduce sliding.

To use the stop, clamp it in its selected position on the fence and hold working stock next to it for sawing. Keep in mind that the clamp does not have as much holding power as a C-clamp. Work carefully and keep a constant eye on the stop to make sure it has not been forced out of position by the workpiece. By using the stop and the measured fence, you will find your measuring job easier, and perhaps even more accurate than ever before.

PROJECT 24: NAIL BOX

Nails are elusive little devils. You invariably buy more than you need for a given project and then put the crumpled sack of leftovers away for "the next time." But when that next time comes, your nails have somehow vanished, and you have to make another trip to the hardware store. If you do find one of those leftover bags, it often contains nails of a size you do not need.

Do you have this problem? If so, this project was designed for you. The nail box shown in Figs. 4-48 and 4-49 uses only scrap lumber, a length of clothesline for the handle, and a dozen or so small nails. See Table 4-9. It will give you practice in making dado cuts on your radial-arm saw and, when you're done, you will have a nail box that you can store almost anyplace until that next time comes.

Notice that it is partitioned into six areas in order to provide room for six sizes or types of nails or other fasteners. When you've completed it, you can round up some of those crumpled sacks. If you can't find any, just buy extra the next time you buy nails.

Making the Cuts

Start by cutting the four sides from the ¾-inch AC plywood scrap (as

Fig. 4-47. This view of the assembled stop shows how it works. The rubber ball tightens the legs against the fence, and the rubber band at the top holds the ball in place when the assembly is not in use. The rubber band at the bottom provides friction between the assembly and the fence in order to reduce slipping possibilities.

Table 4-9. Project 24 Tools.

Saw
Hammer
Countersink Bit
Router
Drill
Measuring Tape

Fig. 4-48. Six different sizes or types of fasteners can be kept in this nailbox to allow you to keep commonly used ones constantly on hand. The rope handle lays flat against the partitions to provide a low-storage profile.

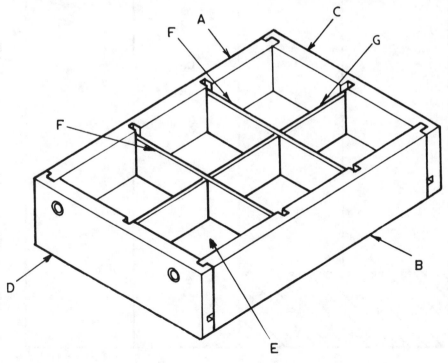

Fig. 4-49. Nail box.

shown in Figs. 4-50 and 4-51). Drill two holes in each end piece (parts C and D) to later receive the rope handle. A countersink bit was used on both sides of the holes to eliminate any chance of cutting and fraying the rope. Then cut parts E, F, and G from quarter-inch plywood stock.

You can use either a router or your radial-arm saw blade to make the various grooves and dadoes that are shown in Fig. 4-52. All of these cuts are of the same depth (⅜ of an inch); one tool setting is all that is required. Repeat cuts with a standard blade in the saw were used to make the illustrated nail box.

To make the cuts, first turn the saw motor so that the blade is set for rip cutting. Measure between the fence and sawblade a distance of ⅜ of an inch and lock the saw into this position. Set the

Fig. 4-50. Nail box cuts.

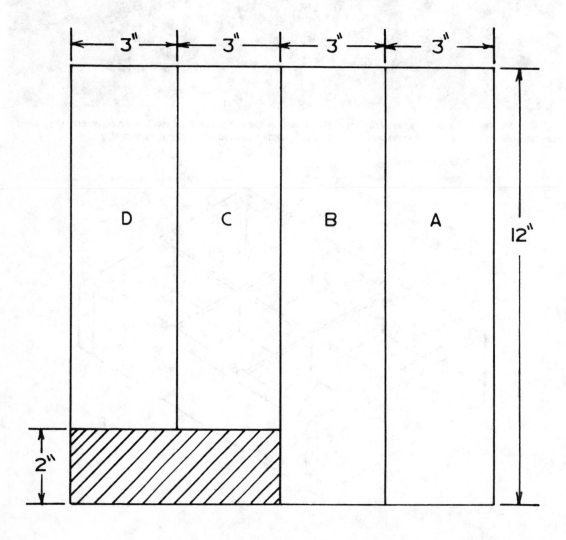

Fig. 4-51. These eight pieces of plywood, that make up the nail box, were derived from scrap lumber. Note placement of various dadoes and grooves.

blade height to ⅜ of an inch above the table surface and make a test cut in a wood scrap to measure for accuracy. When this has been completed, you are ready to make the grooves in parts A, B, C, and D, that will later hold the bottom of the nail box in place. These are made at one time, with the same saw setting, to obtain an accurate fitting.

Start the saw and carefully push each of the four side pieces through it. Then move the saw away from the fence to a distance where the outside of the blade is a fraction over a quarter of an inch from the opposite side of the previous saw kerf. Feed the side pieces through again in the same manner. If there is still uncut wood between these two kerf marks, reset the saw once again to clean it out.

Make the quarter-inch dadoes to receive the "egg crate" partitions. Put parts A and B side by side on your radial-arm saw table, flat and next to the fence, so that the just-cut grooves are facing "up" and are on opposite edges from each other. From the fence outward, there is a ⅜-inch strip of wood, then a groove, then the body of the first side piece, then the second side piece body, then a groove, then a ⅜-inch strip. This placement is made so that, if the next dado is slightly to one side, it will still match the other piece and the partitions inserted later between the two side pieces will remain parallel to each other.

Move the two pieces so that the saw blade, which is still ⅜ of an inch from the table surface, will make a cross cut at 4 inches from the right end. Make this cut through both pieces, return the saw to its starting position, and move the two pieces to the right to prepare for the second cut that will complete the dado. If there is still waste between these two cuts, remove it with another pass of the saw blade.

Move the side pieces, still maintaining their side-to-side relationship to each other, so that the saw will cut through at 4 inches from the other end and repeat the above procedure. Make the second cut to the right of the first one and remove any waste between them. Now make the center dado in parts C and D by lining these two parts up (as previously explained) and making the double cut.

To make the egg crate cuts, line up the single part G, with either A or B, and mark where the cuts are to be made. Hold part G against the fence in a vertical position, raise the saw blade so that it will cut to 1¼ inches down from the top edge, and make a double pass. Now hold the two parts F together, against either part C or part D, mark for the two cuts and make those cuts as before.

This nail box is locked together sturdily with rabbeted and dadoed corners. They are easy to make with either a router or a radial-arm saw blade. Make sure you make these cuts on the correct side of the pieces; it is easy to make a mistake. Assuming you are using a radial-arm saw for this operation, leave it at the same depth setting you used for the quarter-inch grooves and dadoes. Turn part A so that the already-made grooves are touching the table surface and the uncut surface is facing the ceiling. Make a mark ⅜ of an inch from each end and remove the stock between the end and this mark with successive passes of the blade. Do the same thing with the other side piece.

Now make two marks at each end of parts C and D: one ⅜ of an inch from the end and the other ¾ of an inch from the end. With successive passes of the blade, remove the waste between the two pencil marks to a depth of ⅜ of an inch. When the thinned end of part A or B is inserted into this latter groove, it should make a square corner.

Assembling the Box

The box is now ready for assembly. Slip the bottom piece E into the grooves in A and B (Figs. 4-52A and 4-52B). If you prefer, put glue into the grooves first to ensure a rigid joint. Now put an end piece onto each end of the assembly, sliding the bottom piece into the groove, and mating the corners of the side and the end pieces A, B,

Fig. 4-52A. Nail box cuts.

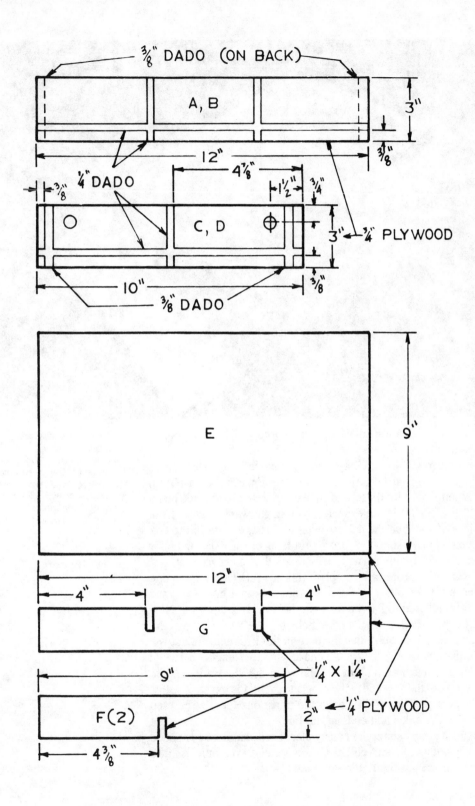

⅜" DADO (ON BACK)

A, B

3"

⅜

12"

4⅞"

1½"

¾"

¼" DADO

⅜"

C, D

3"

¾" PLYWOOD

⊙

⊕

10"

⅜"

⅜" DADO

E

9"

12"

4"

4"

G

¼" X 1¼"

¼" PLYWOOD

9"

F(2)

2"

4⅜"

C, and D. Two or three small nails at each corner will hold this box in its locked position.

Insert part G into the center dadoes in pieces C and D, with the two slots in an upward position. Put the two F parts (Fig. 4-53) in, mating their slots with these, and slide their ends into the side piece dadoes. Although it is not essential, you might want to glue these into place. If you glue the bottom edge of this egg crate to the box floor, you will eliminate any future problems of nails sliding under them and possibly mixing with nails in another compartment.

Inserting the rope will complete this project. Tie a knot in one end and push the other end through one box-end hole from the outside, and then through the opposite hole in the other end. Now feed the rope back through the other hole in the second end, over the partitions, and into the remaining hole in the first end. Adjust the rope so that the knot is snug at the end and the two lengths between the ends will touch each other (as shown in the illustrations). Tie another knot in the free end of the rope and cut off the excess. Notice that the rope will easily lie above the partitions (below the stop surfaces of the sides and ends of the box).

This box can be stored in many places, no clearance is needed for handles. If you do put a pull handle on one end, you could use it to pull the box from a tight storage space.

Fig. 4-52B. Assemble the box just as you would a drawer. The bottom piece need not be glued in if you prefer to allow for expansion. Gluing the egg crate in will, however, keep nails from mixing with those in adjacent compartments.

PROJECT 25: SAW GUIDE AND PROTRACTOR

The most frequent angle you will be called upon to cut in your workshop is 90 degrees (a straight cut). The second most common angle is a 45-degree cut. Both of these are easy to make if you are fortunate enough to have a radial-arm saw. See Table 4-10. If your circular saw is a hand-held one, you must first measure for the cut, mark it, and then somehow keep your saw steady and straight for the cut. A poorly executed cut calls attention to itself on an otherwise professional-looking project.

The protractor shown in Fig. 4-54 will help you perform this vital cutting job skillfully and easily. Not only will it keep your saw straight for 45- or 90-degree angles, it will do so for any angle you are called upon to make. Although it is made of only three pieces of wood, and has absolutely no moving parts, it is a highly versatile tool that is easy to use. It also adds a touch of professionalism.

The accompanying illustrations show how this simple device is used. See Figs 4-55 through 4-57. To make a 45- or 90-degree cut, it is simply held against the wood in T-square fashion so that part B or part C (see Fig. 4-58) is parallel to and touching the work piece. Simply slide the saw along one of its edges to make a near-perfect

Fig. 4-53. Inserting the "egg crate" completes the project. The holes were countersunk before assembly to eliminate rope fraying.

Fig. 4-54. To use the protractor, line up the proper radius line with the workpiece edge, and clamp into place with one C-clamp. The corner of part C, under the far corner in the picture, should be snug against the workpiece.

Fig. 4-55. Use a common protractor to mark 10-degree lines, with the radius hole centered over the mark previously made at corner of part B. Be as accurate as possible because mistakes will be transferred to the workpiece.

Fig. 4-56. Mark 10-degree radius lines with a felt-tip pen held against a yardstick. Move the pen at a steady pace to eliminate blotches of soaked-in ink at points where the pen stops.

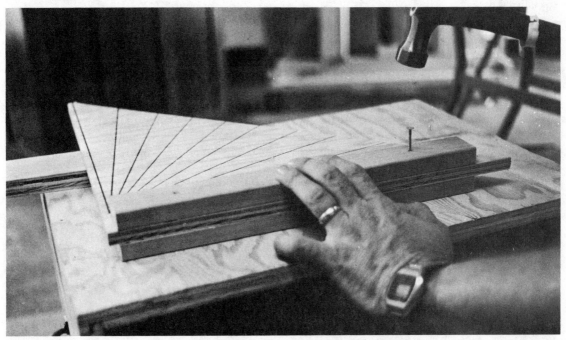

Fig. 4-57. Assemble the protractor with three nails driven into each side. Notice that parts B and C are a quarter inch from the left edge of the protractor body, and their near edges are flush with the protractor base.

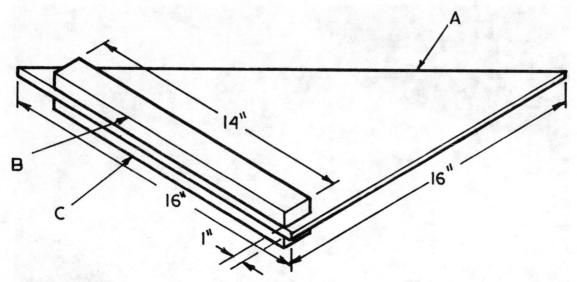

Fig. 4-58. Sawguide and protractor details.

cut. If you want to make the cut with a handsaw, just mark the line, remove the guide, and make the cut.

But what if you wanted to make, for example, a 55-degree angle cut? Notice that the guide has 10 lines on it, radiating from one corner of B (and C). See Figs 4-59 and 4-60. If you put the guide in its standard position for cutting a 45- or 90-degree angle, and then rotate the guide so that the corner of B remains in contact with the workpiece, you are changing the angle of the guide's edge. If you stop this rotation when the line marked 55 degrees is positioned along the edge of the workpiece (as shown in Fig. 4-54) and clamp it into place with a C-clamp, you have automatically determined that angle. You can use your saw along the edge and be confident that it is correct.

The protractor is much more accurate than you might expect as long as care has been taken in drawing the lines. Note, for example, that the distance between the 105 degree and the 115 degree lines, as measured along the 45-degree edge of part A, is relatively long. It is easy enough to interpolate between two lines, find a given point between them (i.e., 110 degrees), and line it up with the edge of the workpiece.

The protractor is made from a piece of half-inch-thick AC plywood. Be very careful to properly mark and cut this piece; all the cuts made from it will reflect any mistakes you make. Use a carpenter's square to make the perpendicular mark for cutting and measure 16 inches from the intersection in both directions. Then lay a straightedge across these two points to determine the hypotenuse of the protractor triangle. The actual cutting of the unit shown in the illustrations was done by the panel saw made in Project 6, which produces extremely accurate cuts.

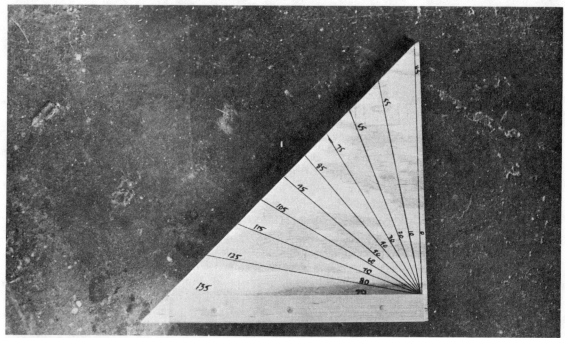

Fig. 4-59. Number your radius lines.

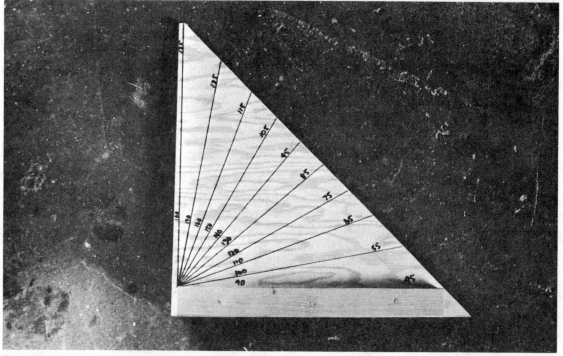

Fig. 4-60. The number along the hypotenuse refer to angles for a saw held along that edge. Numbers closer to the radius center refer to cuts made along the vertical edge.

Lay the triangle on a work surface before you, with the perpendicular side to the left. Place part B or C on the near edge, a quarter inch from the perpendicular edge. After making sure the part's edge is flush with part A's edge, draw around it with a pencil. The upper left corner you have just made is the center point of your protractor.

Now take a large standard protractor, such as found in stationary stores, and lay it on part A so that its center hole is directly over this corner and its base line is directly over the horizontal line you just drew from that corner (Fig. 4-55). Very carefully make a dot at each 10-degree mark around the compass (until reaching the left edge of the wood protractor). Just as carefully, mark a line from the center point through the just-made degree marks; use an accurate straightedge and a fine-tipped felt pen (Fig. 4-56). That completed, place part B in position so that its upper left corner is directly on the center of your array of lines and its closest edge is flush with the edge of part A. Then nail it into place. Perform this same marking and nailing task on the other side of the saw guide and protractor (Fig. 4-57).

Follow Figs. 4-59 and 4-60 to add the correct degree numbers. The outside numbers (those ending in "5") refer to the angle of the saw blade when used along the diagonally cut line. The inside numbers, starting at zero and lying closest to the center point, refer to cuts made along the edge perpendicular to parts B and C.

PROJECT 26: PICTURE FRAME CLAMP

A picture frame is possibly the most frequently made "first project" for home craftsmen. After all, it is relatively easy to make and it is functional. What other beginning project can one hang on his walls for others to admire?

If you have made your own picture frames, you know that "easy to make" is a relative term. If you don't have proper clamps for holding the pieces together while the glue sets, the finished project will be improperly glued (if the pieces stay together at all). See Table 4-11.

The device shown in Fig. 4-61 provides an easy-to-make project that will help you produce those "easy to make" frames with relative ease. It will hold any reasonably sized frame you care to make, and you can make use of materials you might already have on hand. For example, scrap plywood is used for the four corner pieces and fairly common 1-×-2 material is used for the four legs. The only pieces of hardware purchased were two sets of 1½-inch hinges (complete with their own screws). The power for this clamp can come from a variety of sources. Examples are a C-clamp or a gluing clamp.

Start by making the corner pieces as shown in Fig. 4-62. Cut a strip of ¾-inch AC plywood 3 inches wide, and then cut it into eight

Table 4-11. Project 26 Tools.

Saw
Hammer
Screwdriver
Square
Drill
Clamps
Measuring Tape

Fig. 4-61. Almost any size and shape of frame can be made with the picture-frame clamp. A C-clamp or gluing clamp provides the holding power.

Fig. 4-62. Glue and nail the corner blocks together. The countersunk holes are located 1 inch in from two perpendicular sides.

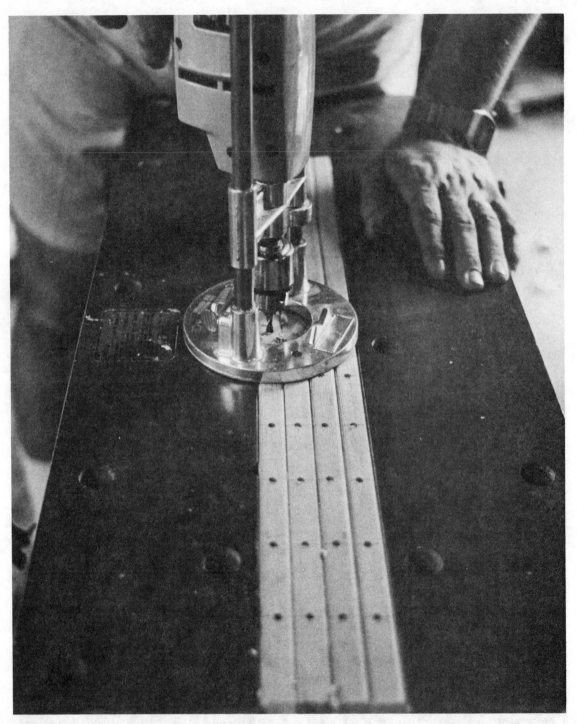

Fig. 4-63. A drill alignment tool is helpful, but not necessary, when drilling holes in the legs. The wood pieces were squeezed together. Then a carpenter's square was used to make pencil marks every 2 inches for hole placement.

Fig. 4-64. Attach hinges to provide the most screw-holding power when they are under clamp pressure.

3-inch-long pieces. Four of these will serve as bases. Drill 5/32-inch holes into them as shown in Fig. 4-62, and cut a quadrant from the other four 3-inch-square pieces. Nail one to each base piece, as shown, and countersink the holes on the top and screw in the flathead machine screws that will later extend down into the legs. Note that a screw-in fit is required.

Cut the four legs from 1-×-2 stock (each one 24 inches long). Clamp them together in your vise or work center (Fig. 4-63); make sure their ends are flush. Use a try-square or a carpenter's square to make cross marks at 2-inch intervals. Then drill a 7/32-inch hole into the center of each board at each pencil mark. You can either drill all the way through or stop the drill before it pierces the other side (as was done in the example).

Cut two 3-inch-long pieces of 1 × 2 and attach the hinges to them as shown in Fig. 4-64. Attach the hinges to the legs and these shorter pieces. Make sure the holes of each set of legs are on the same side after assembly. The hinges are attached contrary to what common sense might dictate. Carefully follow the instructions and carefully examine the photographs.

The picture frame clamp is now ready for use. Cut your picture frame parts, and then determine where the corner assemblies should be located along the legs. Notice that almost any frame size can be accommodated. Because the legs can move up and down, the corners can be positioned every 2 inches along them, and the distance between the two leg sets can vary as far as the C-clamp or gluing clamp will allow.

Apply glue to the frame pieces, and then lay them into the corner blocks. You might want to first apply wax, or waxed paper, into the corners in order to ward off any glue drops that might escape the joint. Place the frame pieces into the corners, adjust the clamp, and then tighten the unit. Allow the glue to dry, and then remove the frame from the clamp.